Music Business Research

Music business research is a new multidisciplinary field that puts a number of different analytical approaches into mutual dialogue. It is located at the intersection of economic, artistic, musical, cultural, social, legal, and technological understandings of this cultural industry and it aims to generate a better understanding of the creation, distribution and consumption of music as a cultural good. As a field it is therefore characterised by methodological diversity and involves linking academic research with music business practices. The book series welcomes monographs and edited volumes that feature groundbreaking research into this dynamic and exciting field.

Michaela Drnek Bóková

Strategies of Micro-Enterprises in the Recording Industry

How Independent Jazz Labels Navigate the Music Landscape

Springer

Michaela Drnek Bóková
Janáček Academy of Performing Arts
Brno, Czech Republic

ISSN 2522-0829 ISSN 2522-0837 (electronic)
Music Business Research
ISBN 978-3-031-88438-2 ISBN 978-3-031-88439-9 (eBook)
https://doi.org/10.1007/978-3-031-88439-9

This Springer imprint is published by the registered company Springer Nature Switzerland AG
The registered company address is: Gewerbestrasse 11, 6330 Cham, Switzerland

List of Informants

Representatives of Digital Distribution Companies

Kervin M. Dockendorf/Fangtasia Music (DE)

Kervin Alberto Martinez Dockendorf is a creative entrepreneur and the founder and managing director of the digital distribution company Fangtasia Music based in Germany. Dockendorf has over nine years of experience as an employee in the "formal" music industry and more than seventeen years of experience as a freelancer/entrepreneur in the independent music industry, working with catalogs, rights management, royalties, record labels, music publishers, and booking/management agencies.

In 2016, he started his own company, Fangtasia Music, which delivers music and video distribution services to labels, bands, and artists (provided by Kervin M. Dockendorf, 2024).

Kyle McEvoy (USA)

Kyle McEvoy, an upstate New York-based multi-instrumentalist, songwriter, and producer, brings a wealth of experience from touring with notable artists like Mac DeMarco and Cage the Elephant to serving as the lead guitarist for Kath Bloom. He has contributed his songwriting and production talents to various artists, including The Shivers and Peter CottonTale. He is the CEO of the independent label and distribution company Sonder House and Only One on the Mountain, is co-owner of Cloverdale Records, and has held A&R and label manager positions at Chillhop Music, Nettwerk, and Pickup Music (provided by Kyle McEvoy, 2024).

McEvoy's efforts in music marketing, distribution, and label policy have secured him and some of his fellows over a million monthly listeners on Spotify (Spotify, 2024).

Naemi Wetter/The Orchard (DE)

Naemi Wetter currently holds the position of Label Manager at The Orchard in Hamburg, Germany, a role she has held for over three years. The Orchard is a leading music distribution company, operating in over 40 markets worldwide and providing a comprehensive suite of artist and label services, including full-service marketing, sync licensing, video services, data analysis, advertising, rights management, and both digital and physical distribution.

Prior to her tenure at The Orchard, Wetter gained experience in music publishing as Copyright Assistant at ROBA Music Publishing for 1.5 years. She holds a Bachelor's degree in Popular Music and Media from the University of Paderborn. Additionally, Wetter serves as Product Manager for several independent artists, including Hayien, Artisblind, and Katzi. Her work spans both corporate and creative aspects of the music industry (provided by Naemi Wetter, 2024).

All three representatives of the distribution companies have collaborated with jazz artists, but their experiences include a wide variety of artists and genres.

Representatives of Independent Jazz Record Labels

ACT Music (DE)/Andreas Brandis

ACT Music, a German label renowned for its diverse lineup of top-tier jazz instrumentalists and vocalists, has significantly influenced contemporary jazz with its releases. Founded in 1992 by music manager and producer Siggi Loch, ACT Music has established a global presence and reputation. Its impressive roster features artists such as the Esbjörn Svensson Trio, Nils Landgren, Michael Wollny, Marius Neset, Lars Danielsson, Joachim Kühn, Ulf Wakenius, Youn Sun Nah, Nguyên Lê, Leszek Możdżer, Vincent Peirani, Émile Parisien, and many others. While primarily focusing on European jazz, ACT Music has also been pivotal in advancing the careers of US artists like Terri Lyne Carrington, David Binney, Vince Mendoza, Vijay Iyer, and Rudresh Mahanthappa. With over 500 albums released, ACT Music continues to shape the jazz genre, adhering to its mission of presenting music "in the spirit of jazz" (ACT Music, 2024).

Andreas Brandis, a German music producer and executive, is currently the CEO and a shareholder of ACT Music and Vision. With a background in classical percussion, jazz drums, and music education, Brandis brings extensive experience from international ensembles and theaters. He has held significant roles in major music companies, including ECM, Universal Music Group, and Deutsche Grammophon. Brandis also founded The ACT Agency, which manages artist careers and produces concerts. Additionally, he teaches artist development and music business at various institutions (Brandis, 2024).

Enja Records (DE)/Werner Aldinger

Enja Records is a German jazz record company and label based in Munich founded by jazz enthusiasts Matthias Winckelmann and Horst Weber in 1971. The label's first release was by Mal Waldron, and early releases included European and Japanese avant-garde artists such as Alexander von Schlippenbach, Terumasa Hino, Albert Mangelsdorff, and Yosuke Yamashita, along with newer American jazz musicians like Archie Shepp, Cecil Taylor, Leroy Jenkins, and Eric Dolphy and straight-ahead musicians such as Tommy Flanagan, McCoy Tyner, Chet Baker, Freddie Hubbard, Elvin Jones, and Kenny Barron. The label also branched out to release early world music productions from Abdullah Ibrahim, Rabih Abou-Khalil, Mahmoud Turkmani, Gypsy bands, Indonesia's Monica Akihary, and Turkish saz virtuoso Taner Akyol (Wikipedia, 2019).

Werner Aldinger is a significant figure in the jazz music industry, particularly noted for his roles as a label manager and producer. In the early 1980s, he played in bands such as Embryo and Dissidenten and worked with Charlie Mariano and Schäggy Bädsch. From 1987 to 1989, Aldinger hosted music and youth programs for Bayerischer Rundfunk, including "Rocklok," "Nachtsession," and "Zündfunk." He also contributed articles to various jazz and hi-fi magazines. In 1990, Horst Weber brought him to Enja Records as a label manager and producer. Ten years later, Aldinger took over Weber's role. In 2008, he established his own label, Yellowbird Records (Wikipedia, 2021). Aldinger's productions have received multiple awards, including the Preis der deutschen Schallplattenkritik (German Record Critics' Award) for works by Jun Miyake, Elliott Sharp, Aki Takase, Paul Brody, Archie Shepp, Mal Waldron, and Roman Bunka. His work has also been recognized with the Echo Jazz award. As a producer, he has collaborated with artists such as Dewey and Joshua Redman, Sun Ra, Eddie Harris, Myra Melford, Marc Ribot, Johannes Enders, Michel Godard, Nils Wogram, Lucia Cadotsch, Roy Nathanson, David Liebman, and Kip Hanrahan (ibid).

Freifeld Tontraeger (AT)/Alexander Yannilos

Freifeld Tontraeger is an independent music label based in Vienna, Austria, focused on progressive and experimental music. The label was founded by Alexander Yannilos, who also produces, records, mixes, and masters many of its projects. Freifeld Tontraeger supports a wide range of music genres, including jazz, pop, experimental club music, and live electronics (Freifeld Tontraeger, 2022).

One notable initiative under Freifeld Tontraeger is the Fraufeld project, which aims to promote female composers and musicians. The first album in this series, "Fraufeld Vol. 1," was released in 2017 and features a diverse array of female artists and composers (ibid).

Alexander Yannilos is an Austrian drummer, vocalist, and music producer born in Vienna in 1989. He has been involved in numerous projects spanning jazz, contemporary music, pop, experimental club music, and live electronics. Yannilos founded the music collective MOTHERDRUM and co-founded the Freifeld Association and its label, Freifeld Tontraeger. He has received several awards, including the Startstipendium for Music, and participated in The New Austrian Sound of Music program. Yannilos has produced over seventy albums and collaborated with various artists on the Austrian scene and beyond (Wien Modern, 2022).

Greenleaf Music (USA)/Dave Douglas

Greenleaf Music is an independent music label founded by the renowned trumpeter and composer Dave Douglas in 2005. The label is dedicated to supporting artists fully and fairly, offering a platform for a diverse range of jazz and improvised music. Greenleaf Music produces CDs, digital downloads, and sheet music and offers a subscription service that provides exclusive content to its members (Greenleaf Music, 2005–2024).

The label's roster features a variety of talented artists, including Mareike Wiening, Itamar Borochov, and the Webber/Morris Big Band, among others. Greenleaf Music is known for its innovative approach to jazz, blending traditional elements with contemporary and experimental sounds. Dave Douglas, the driving force behind the label, continues to release his own projects through Greenleaf, such as the acclaimed "Gifts" album (ibid).

In addition to producing music, Greenleaf Music engages with its audience through a blog, a podcast series titled "A Noise from the Deep," and regular Q&A sessions with artists. This multifaceted approach has helped Greenleaf Music establish a strong community of jazz enthusiasts and musicians (ibid).

Dave Douglas is a prolific trumpeter, composer, educator, and entrepreneur from New York City. He is known for the stylistic breadth of his work and for keeping a diverse set of ensembles and projects active simultaneously. His contributions to improvised music have garnered distinguished recognition, including a Guggenheim Fellowship, an Aaron Copland Award, and two GRAMMY® nominations. While his career spans more than forty recordings as a leader, his active projects include his Quintet Sound Prints, a band co-led with saxophonist Joe Lovano; Riverside, a quartet co-led with Chet Doxas; a duo with pianist Uri Caine; and debuting in 2015, High Risk, an electronic music-influenced quartet with Mark Guiliana, Jonathan Maron, and Shigeto (ibid).

Since 2005, Douglas has operated his own record label, Greenleaf Music, releasing his own recordings as well as albums by other artists in the jazz idiom. Through his artist-friendly approach and innovative practices, he continues to prove himself a pioneer among artist-run labels (ibid).

Heartcore Records (DE)/Kurt Rosenwinkel

Heartcore Records, founded by jazz guitarist, composer, and producer Kurt Rosenwinkel, is an independent record label dedicated to releasing high-quality music across all genres. Established in 2016 in Berlin, Germany, with support from Eric Clapton and other backers, the label has since released numerous albums and initiated various educational and beneficial projects. Heartcore Records aims not only to promote top-tier music and support promising artists in realizing their visions but also to contribute to society through various philanthropic initiatives (Heartcore Records, 2023).

The label's vision is to "create a brand that celebrates the deep connection of the human spirit beyond any genre or category, acknowledging that all musical traditions are interconnected. The name 'Heartcore' reflects this philosophy, symbolizing music created with heart, from the core, and with complete dedication." Besides Rosenwinkel himself, the label releases music of Pedro Martins, Daniel Santiago, Lucia Cadotsch, Cecil Alexander, and many other international artists (ibid).

Kurt Rosenwinkel is a renowned jazz guitarist, composer, and bandleader, acclaimed as one of the most influential musicians of his generation. With a career spanning over 30 years, Rosenwinkel has released numerous notable albums and collaborated with a wide range of established artists. His innovative approach to composition and improvisation has earned him a distinguished reputation among music enthusiasts and continues to inspire emerging musicians (Kurt Rosenwinkel, 2023).

Hevhetia (SK)/Ján Súdzina

Hevhetia is an independent Slovak record label founded in 2001. The label's mission is to promote and distribute high-quality music produced by Slovak and foreign artists in various genres, such as jazz, world music, classical music, and avant-garde (Hevhetia, 2023).

Hevhetia has established itself as one of the most prominent and active record labels in the Slovak music scene, and it has been instrumental in promoting Slovak music abroad. The label has released over 200 albums, including works by renowned Slovak artists such as Peter Lipa, Juraj Griglak, and Lucia Lužinská, as well as international musicians such as John Abercrombie, Miroslav Vitous, and Enrico Rava. The label has also organized various concerts, festivals, and other events to promote its music and showcase the talent of its artists. Hevhetia is managed by economist, cultural manager, journalist, and music enthusiast Ján Súdzina (ibid).

Ján Súdzina is a key figure in the Slovak music industry, primarily known for founding the Hevhetia record label in 2001. Hevhetia focuses on minority music genres such as jazz, blues, alternative, and experimental music. Under Súdzina's leadership, Hevhetia has published over 350 music titles from artists in more than

50 countries, including collaborations with musicians from France, Israel, Korea, Ukraine, Norway, Austria, and Poland (Danko, 2021). Súdzina has also been involved in organizing the Hevhetia Summer Music Festival since 2011, which became international in 2015, hosting events in Slovakia, the Czech Republic, Hungary, Poland, and France. Additionally, he was the executive director of the European Capital of Culture 2013 project in Košice from 2011 to 2014 and serves as the president of the Košice Marathon Club (ibid).

Ma Records (CZ)/Vojta Drnek

Ma Records is an independent label specializing in jazz, improvised, and experimental music, representing a community of Czech musicians dedicated to these genres. The label aims to introduce the creative work of artists who have ventured beyond easily categorizable musical boundaries. Ma Records primarily releases albums on Bandcamp, occasionally offering physical formats as well. The label's goal is to raise awareness of a scene they deeply believe in, supporting free, intuitive, and authentic artistic expression. The name "Ma" is derived from Japanese aesthetics, philosophy, and art, symbolizing the fusion of time and space where something new emerges from pure energy. It represents the potential for free, intuitive, and authentic artistic expression, creating a space for innovation between established forms and genres (Bandcamp, 2020).

Vojta Drnek is a Czech accordionist and composer based in Berlin, known for his wide-ranging musical repertoire that includes swing, mainstream jazz, modern jazz, contemporary performances, and free improvisation. Drnek leads and participates in various bands and projects. In addition to his performance career, Vojta Drnek co-founded Ma Records in 2021, a label dedicated to jazz, experimental, and improvised music, alongside saxophonist and composer Michal Wroblewski (Vojta Drnek, 2023). Wroblewski is a versatile saxophonist and composer recognized for his work in jazz and contemporary music (Bandcamp, 2020).

Razdaz Recordz (USA)/Ray Jefford

Razdaz Recordz was founded in New York City in 2002 by internationally acclaimed bassist, singer, and composer Avishai Cohen with his manager Ray Jefford. Razdaz has established itself as a key independent record label, bringing young artistic talent to the forefront of the music industry with the help of its close global partners. With Razdaz Recordz, Avishai created an opportunity to record and produce young, talented musicians for whom he is enthusiastic. His vision behind the label was to give himself an outlet to creatively express the diversity of his musical journey, eclecticism, and artistic passion (Razdaz Recordz, 2023).

Razdaz Recordz produces and presents an eclectic mix of genres, ranging from Middle-Eastern vibes to wild techno beats, from jazz rhythms to soulful vocal albums, always taking into account the artists' own personal ambitions and their own definitive message (ibid).

Ray Jefford is a music manager known for his work with renowned Israeli jazz bassist Avishai Cohen. Formerly in sales management, Jefford transitioned to music management after meeting Cohen through Chick Corea in New York. Over two decades, Jefford and Cohen developed a close professional relationship, launching Razdaz Recordz to support Cohen's music and other emerging artists (Samkova, 2020).

We Jazz Records (FIN)/Matti Nives

We Jazz Records is a Helsinki-based label known for presenting cutting-edge and innovative jazz from Northern Europe. The label is renowned for its eclectic range, spanning no-nonsense straight-ahead swing to ambient-tinged electronic experiments. "The 'jazz' in We Jazz encompasses many different styles," says founder Matti Nives. Established as a festival in Helsinki in 2013, the We Jazz label was launched in 2016. Nives primarily focuses on Finnish bands, featuring acclaimed musicians like Timo Lassy, Jukka Eskola, Teppo Mäkynen, and Jukka Perko, experimental projects by Mopo and Bowman Trio, and international artists such as Otis Sandsjö, Petter Eldh, and Brooklyn-based baritone saxophonist Jonah Parzen-Johnson (Bandcamp, 2023).

Matti Nives is a versatile figure in the jazz music scene, serving as a DJ, broadcaster, designer, writer, and music curator. Based in Helsinki, Finland, Nives is the founder and artistic director of We Jazz Records. He began his career as a DJ in 2005 and has been actively involved in radio, hosting shows such as "Lauantaijatsit" on Bassoradio and "Jazz kiinnostaa," "Matti Nives," and "Avantgardeyö" on Radio Helsinki. His dedication to Finnish jazz culture was recognized in 2011 when Yle's Jazzradio awarded him the Varjo-Yrjö accolade. In addition to his work with We Jazz Records, Nives launched an experimental music program on Yle Radio 1 called "Frekvenssi" in 2021. This program explores various aspects of experimental music, particularly electronic music, aiming to transcend genre boundaries. Nives also serves as the artistic advisor for the Helsinki Festival and the program manager for G Livelab Helsinki (Jazz Finland, 2021).

Acknowledgments

I want to give a heartfelt thank you to my tutor, doc. Ing. MgA. Lucie Pešl Šilerová, PhD, and my advisor, Mgr. Vít Kouřil, for their guidance and insightful feedback throughout this journey. Thanks to the Janáček Academy of Performing Arts, my alma mater, for providing a warm home to my complete academic education and supporting this research.

My sincere thanks to Kurt Rosenwinkel for his support and for giving me the opportunity to manage and build Heartcore Records. The invaluable experience I've gained while working with him has been a major asset to this study. I extend my thanks to all the interviewees who generously shared their expertise and insights.

Special thanks to my husband and working partner, Vojta Drnek, whose continuous support and understanding mean the world to me.

Last but not least, to my family and friends all over the world, thank you all for always encouraging me to pursue my dreams. Your love and friendship have been and will always be my foundation.

Michaela

Competing Interests The author has no competing interests to declare that are relevant to the content of this manuscript.

About This Book

The book *Strategies of Micro-Enterprises in the Recording Industry: How Independent Jazz Labels Navigate the Music Landscape* examines the strategies of micro-enterprises in the recording industry, specifically focusing on independent jazz record labels. The book provides a comprehensive analysis of the current state and future prospects of these small-scale entities in the context of the rapidly evolving digital music landscape. Through a combination of desk research and semi-structured interviews with representatives from independent jazz labels and digital distribution companies, the research identifies key strategies in financial management, product development, distribution, and marketing.

The findings reveal how independent jazz micro-labels navigate the challenges posed by the dominance of streaming services. Despite limited resources, these labels demonstrate innovative approaches to sustaining their business and promoting their artists. The study highlights the importance of community building, digital marketing, and the strategic use of digital distribution tools in achieving financial sustainability and market presence.

This research contributes to the understanding of independent music production and offers practical recommendations for micro-enterprises in the jazz recording sector to thrive in the digital age.

Introduction

Jazz and the recording industry both emerged in the late nineteenth and early twentieth centuries. Before jazz was introduced, the music industry focused mainly on popular genres like opera. Jazz, with its improvisational style, was largely ignored because "music publishers and phonographic companies had not enough use for the improvised musical forms of Jazz" (Tschmuck, 2006, p. 51). In 1917, the Original Dixieland Jass Band produced the first jazz recording, *Livery Stable Blues,* a significant milestone in music history (Vigil, 2022). However, jazz developed far from the main centers of music publishing and recording, particularly in New Orleans, which lagged behind the rest of the country in developing the phonographic industry.

Today, over a century after its first recording, jazz continues to evolve and face new challenges. With the rapid advancement in technology and the shift toward digital music consumption, jazz musicians and jazz businesses must constantly adapt to stay relevant. The streaming era has introduced new models of financing, production, distribution, and marketing. Finding a place on streaming services amidst countless genres and millions of tracks has become a modern-day struggle for jazz artists. Yet, this resilient genre persists, continually reinventing itself and finding innovative ways to reach new audiences.

This book deals with the present situation of independent jazz micro-labels and examines their current and future organizational strategies. The author defines the basic concepts that place the issue in the context of the independent recording industry and describes the contemporary events associated with changes in music economics, product, distribution, and marketing. It explains the conditions for independent micro-labels in jazz, seeking financial sustainability and a place in the worldwide market of recorded music.

Even though the jazz genre is no longer the mainstream matter it used to be in the first half of the twentieth century (Raffa, 2017, p. 69), its tradition lingers on in many forms, inciting the foundations of new dedicated communities, schools, venues, festivals, publishing entities, independent record labels, online blogs, social media groups, and much more (Prouty, 2012). This research is focused solely on the independent jazz labels that operate with less than ten employees.

The motivations driving "do-it-yourself" (hereinafter referred to as DIY) micro-independents to immerse themselves in music production frequently manifest as political or moral convictions, as expounded by Rosen (1997), Hesmondhalgh (1998b), and Strachan (2007). Positioned as a resistance against the dominant capitalist discourse dominated by major record companies, these independents endeavor to transform or democratize the prevailing system, ultimately promoting counter-hegemonic or non-mainstream genres, often encapsulated under the umbrella of "indie" genres. By releasing genres outside the mainstream, these small record companies not only carve out a niche but also contribute to the diversification of contemporary music. The interactive nature of the Internet further amplifies this impact, facilitating the dissemination and promotion of music. Despite their limited scale, DIY micro-independents strive to influence music consumption, engaging in public debates on musical taste, thereby challenging the dominance of major players in the commercial music industry (Hitters & den Drijver, 2017, pp. 31-33).

There are various reasons why such organizations/companies come to live. Some entrepreneurs want to find a way to a stable income, and some want to have a loyal fan base. Some are purely about creating an independent platform for an artist or/and a community, and others invest in their business as a hobby (Sect. 4.2.1 "Goals and Visions"). In every case, these goals need to be fulfilled by financial investments in the production, manufacture[1], distribution, and marketing of digital and physical music albums, audio, audiovisual content, and more (Macy et al. 2016). This research asks what the micro-entrepreneurs' strategies are for financing, distribution, and marketing their products and sustaining their ongoing business in the current environment.

Today's business models offer these companies a variety of tools for placing their products on the global music market in physical and especially digital form, which significantly increases the number of newly created digital music labels, one-man labels, and DIY artists who have decided to omit the label as an intermediary. At the same time, however, the labels and these independent artists are finding themselves in a highly competitive environment, and to exist in the world of streaming music, they are forced to accept the terms of streaming platforms, which are currently still looking for a way to distribute artistic fees fairly via organizational changes and price optimization (Smith & Telang, 2017).

Having worked as a label manager deeply entrenched in the nuances of the music industry, I've directly observed the challenges jazz artists encounter in garnering visibility and acknowledgment on streaming platforms. Their struggles with the platforms' algorithms and promotional methods inspired me to thoroughly explore this issue. Hence, this book is born out of a genuine interest in exploring and addressing the systemic hurdles that hinder the widespread recognition of jazz music in the digital sphere. Ultimately, my aim is to cultivate a more fair and inclusive landscape for jazz musicians in the era of streaming.

[1] Only if physical carrier and/or merchandising are considered.

The opening chapter sets the stage by presenting the key questions driving the study and explaining the methods used to gather relevant data.

The second chapter, "Basic Terms Definition," serves as a fundamental guide, clarifying essential terms to provide a comprehensive understanding within a broader context. This section includes a concise historical overview and the current state of the recording industry and the jazz genre.

The third chapter, "Findings," reveals the insights gained from interviews with those informants. The section offers the perspective of three informants who represent independent digital distributors and comment on the trends and challenges related to today's and future music industry practices. The chapter then investigates various aspects of independent jazz micro-labels, including their financial mechanisms, distribution channels, marketing methodologies, and strategic responses to the increasing dominance of streaming services, based on interviews with nine informants who represent these labels. Additionally, it explores their perspectives on the dynamic realm of marketing in the streaming era and examines their alignment with current market trends.

In the following chapter, "Conclusion and Discussion," the author summarizes the information obtained from the semi-structured interviews to collect information on the strategic choices of independent jazz micro-labels in financial activities, distribution, marketing, and product development within the contemporary music industry. The chapter "Conclusion and Discussion" shows the results of the interviews, detailing the characteristics of these niche entities and their responses to the market shift at the turn of the century (IFPI, 2024). It investigates whether these micro-labels perceive this market shift and their subsequent reactions. Additionally, it examines the assertion by Dias and Medbøe (2014) that the jazz genre resists technological change, exploring current adaptations by independent micro-labels to an evolving industry. The research also delves into the awareness and utilization of streaming service tools and strategies by these labels, evaluating their engagement with digital resources to enhance their market presence.

The final chapters, "Research Limitations" and "Personal Observations," outline the study's scope and methodological limitations and suggest areas for future research. Additionally, they provide the author's perspective on the research process and personal insights and ideas related to the study.

Contents

About the Author

MgA. Michaela Drnek Bóková, PhD, is a Czech music manager, producer, and vocalist based in Berlin, Germany. She earned her PhD from the Janáček Academy of Music in Brno (JAMU).

Since 2016, she has been the founding manager of legendary jazz guitarist and composer Kurt Rosenwinkel's record label Heartcore Records in Berlin. In this position, she covers multiple roles related to creative project management and production, artist management, business planning, and record label branding.

Michaela's career is distinguished by her *forward-thinking projects* and *philanthropic initiatives*. In 2017, she launched "Heartcore for the World," an initiative teaching and recording children from challenging environments, aiming to provide underprivileged children and youths with access to music education.

Michaela also lectures at JAMU, teaching a specialized course on independent record label processes, merging theory with real-world applications from her industry experience.

Outside of her academic and managerial duties, Michaela continues to contribute to the artistic community through her work as a vocalist, often collaborating on jazz, experimental and cross-genre projects. In 2023, she appeared on stage at Eric Clapton's Guitar Crossroads in LA, joining Kurt Rosenwinkel's band as a performer.

Abbreviations

AI	Artificial intelligence
ADA	Alternative Distribution Alliance
CD	Compact disc
DIY	Do-it-yourself
DSP	Digital service providers
D2F	Direct-to-fan
ECM	Edition of Contemporary Music
ERA	Entertainment and Retail Association
EU	European Union
FPU	Fund for Arts Support (FPU - Fond na podporu umenia), Slovakia
IAM	International Association for Jazz Education
IFPI	International Federation of the Phonographic Industry
LP	Long play (vinyl record)
MSS	Music streaming services
ODJB	Original Dixieland Jass Band
PR	Public relations
P2P	Peer-to-peer
RIAA	Recording Industry Association of America
SEO	Search engine optimization
SAE	School of Audio Engineering
SME (in the context of major record labels)	Sony Music Entertainment
SME (in the context of enterprise size definition)	Small and medium enterprise
UMG	Universal Music Group
WMG	Warner Music Group

List of Figures

List of Tables

Chapter 1
Research Questions and Description of the Research Plan

Abstract This chapter outlines the framework of the study, presenting its objectives, research questions, and methodological approach. It details the methods employed, including desk research and qualitative interviews, and defines the criteria and processes used to gather and analyze data. The chapter also provides an overview of the relevant literature on the topic, reviewing key publications that have addressed the subject in the past. Additionally, it briefly introduces the respondents and offers a more detailed description of the companies they are involved with. This establishes the structure of the research and lays a solid foundation for investigating the strategies and challenges faced by independent jazz micro-labels.

1.1 Objectives of the Research

The goal of the research is to: (a) describe current events in the recording industry with a focus on independent jazz micro-labels, (b) map and evaluate the current situation in independent jazz micro-labels, and (c) if applicable, suggest effective strategic procedures for independent jazz micro-labels. These assessments and recommendations should be useful for improving their conditions in the future.

In this study, the researcher has selected three representatives of digital music distributors and nine micro record labels operating across diverse territories in the EU and U.S.A., each featuring an artist roster comprising international talent. Despite their geographical diversity, these labels encounter similar challenges in distributing and promoting their productions on a global scale.

M. Drnek Bóková, *Strategies of Micro-Enterprises in the Recording Industry*, Music Business Research, https://doi.org/10.1007/978-3-031-88439-9_1

1.2 Summary of Questions and Research Topics

a. **What are the characteristics of independent jazz micro-labels?**

By focusing on the characteristics specific to jazz, a niche genre with its distinct challenges and opportunities, the research aims to uncover the nuanced strategies employed by these labels for survival and growth. The investigation into the characteristics of these labels is not only crucial for shedding light on their role in the global independent music market but also for providing insights into how they navigate the challenges posed by digitalization, streaming services, and evolving consumer preferences.

b. **What product, distribution, marketing, and financial strategies do the independent micro-companies in jazz choose for their activities?**

This question focuses on a complex understanding of the specific choices made by these small-scale entities across key areas such as financial strategies, product offerings, distribution channels, and marketing approaches. Surveying these strategic decisions is essential for gaining insights into how these micro-companies navigate the intricate environment of the music industry, providing a detailed perspective on their adaptive measures and business models and offering practical implications for industry practitioners, aspiring label owners, and policymakers, adding value to the ongoing dialogue surrounding the dynamics of independent jazz micro-labels within the music industry.

b1: Dias and Medbøe (2014b) claim that representatives of the jazz genre lag and even resist change and are unwilling to adapt to evolving technological progress. What do the independent jazz micro-labels do today to adapt to the ever-changing industry?

b2: There are multiple streaming services "handbooks" advising multiple tips and strategies for effective releases in the digital environment (Greenwood, 2023b, Other Records Labels, 2022b). Are the independent jazz micro-labels aware of the available tools, and are they using them?

1.3 Research Methods

To understand the strategies of independent jazz micro-labels, the author used both qualitative and quantitative methods. Desk research allowed for a comprehensive review of existing literature and statistics, while semi-structured interviews provided firsthand niche industry insights. This mixed-methods approach combines broad data review with detailed qualitative insights. Despite the subjective nature of interviews, these methods together offer a well-rounded framework for analyzing the industry's complexities.

Table 1.1 The overview of research questions (the author)

Research question	Methodology	Details
What are the characteristics of independent jazz micro-labels?	Desk research, semi-structured interviews	Analyzing existing literature and industry reports and conducting interviews with label representatives.
What financial, product, distribution, and marketing strategies do the independent jazz micro-companies choose for their activities?	Semi-structured interviews	Interviews focused on strategy topics, supplemented by secondary data from industry publications.
How do independent jazz micro-labels adapt to the ever-changing industry?	Desk research, semi-structured interviews	Literature review on industry trends, interviews exploring adaptation strategies.

The chapter on research methods explains the methodologies employed in constructing the framework for this study. The initial stages, encompassed in the chapter titled "Basic Terms Definition" heavily leaned on desk research, drawing insights from academic and popular literature to establish foundational knowledge.

The Findings chapter adopted a dual methodology, incorporating both desk research and semi-structured interviews. While desk research facilitated a thorough examination of the labels' online presence, historical evolution, and product offerings, the inclusion of semi-structured interviews added another dimension, capturing firsthand insights from industry practitioners.

The primary source for the desk research was content analysis, which involved researching music business-related literature, research papers, articles, annual reports, and websites. These sources have served as an informative tool for the qualitative data about jazz independent record labels in the music industry. The author also used statistics to support the complex analysis of the music industry with quantitative data.

It's worth noting that certain methods, such as experimental research and surveys, were deliberately excluded, given the qualitative nature of the study and the nuanced insights sought from industry experts. This chapter unravels the intricacies of the chosen methodologies, shedding light on their appropriateness and limitations in the pursuit of a comprehensive analysis of the strategies employed by independent jazz micro-labels in the recording industry. The methodology is designed to comprehensively address the research questions (Table 1.1).

1.3.1 Desk Research

Previous Studies and Publications on the Given Topic

Numerous studies have been conducted on the recording industry and independent record labels and their impact on the music industry, but there is a lack of research specifically focused solely on the jazz genre in relation to the recording industry. Some of the publications include jazz-focused labels in their research as a chapter, as in *Labels: Making Independent Music* (Bartmanski & Woodward, 2020b). The writers of this chapter focused particularly on labels that entered independent music, mostly electronic music, after 2000. The book extensively uses interviews conducted with labels including Ostgut Ton in Berlin, Argot in Chicago, 100% Silk in Los Angeles, Ninja Tune in London, and Goma Gringa in Sao Paulo and served as an inspiration for this study. The authors interviewed 40 respondents from 37 organizations and recorded the variety of models and approaches of independent businesses. They explain the parameters of independence and discuss the material and symbolic economy of small record labels. They also explain the aspects and show examples of urban ecology in relation to the electronic music scene and club culture (Bartmanski & Woodward, 2020b).

A study, *Independent Cultural Production: The Case of a Jazz Recording Company* (Gray, 1983b), was built on research on one specific independent jazz record label and its functioning. According to Gray, a recording company's independence is determined by its work, records, creative answers to its environment, the devotion of its workers, and organizational philosophy rather than by its structural and economic conditions. The founders of Theresa Records, who are the informants for this study, explain how remaining a small business allows them to produce only the music they support and avoid having a hierarchical organizational structure. Nevertheless, being a micro-company has its drawbacks when it comes to establishing a name, collecting accounts receivable, and securing cash flow for the next production (Gray, 1983b). The insights from Gray's study, conducted over three decades ago, serve as a reminder of the evolving nature of independent jazz recording companies and the importance of reflecting on current challenges and opportunities in contemporary research.

As an inspiration for the chapter about the label's goals served the paper "The Business of DIY: Characteristics, Motives, and Ideologies of Micro-Independent Record Labels" (Hitters & den Drijver, 2017b). Notably, the conclusion of their work contributes to a deeper understanding of cultural production practices in the nondominant music industry of the Netherlands. In a landscape where prior research predominantly hails from the United Kingdom or the United States, their study uniquely explores the Dutch micro-independent scene, uncovering motivations and practices distinct from those observed in Anglo-Saxon contexts. The absence of political motives among Dutch micro-independents, as highlighted by the authors, underscores the nuanced differences that may exist across diverse cultural and industry landscapes. This paper's exploration of uncharted territories and the influence of global music market dynamics opens avenues for further inquiry, especially concerning the varying influences of creative industries, political and cultural policies, local art ecosystems, and socio-economic factors in different countries (Hitters & den Drijver, 2017b, 17–35).

A very important source for this study was the paper "Improvisation in the Digital Age: New Narratives in Jazz Promotion and Dissemination" by José Dias and Haftor Medbøe (Dias & Medbøe, 2014b). It explores the significant shifts in the jazz music industry brought about by the digital revolution. It highlights the decline in support from major labels and the rise of independent, often musician-led, labels.

Despite the democratization of music distribution through digital platforms like iTunes and Spotify, many independent releases struggle due to limited marketing resources. The paper discusses how musicians have adopted DIY strategies, such as free download netlabels and interactive app albums, to navigate the challenges of promotion and dissemination in an overcrowded market. It emphasizes the necessity for innovative approaches to ensure the sustainability and growth of jazz in the contemporary digital landscape.

There is available literature describing the complex functions of the recording industry, such as *The Economics of Music* (Tschmuck, 2021b), *Rethinking the Music Business* (Morgen, 2022), and *The Music Business and Recording Industry* (Hutchison et al., 2011). However, these sources mostly focus on the data of major record companies and do not delve deep into the independent sector.

Another publication covering the recording industry is *Creativity and Innovation in the Music Industry* (Tschmuck, 2006b). The book traverses twentieth-century music industry history, particularly focusing on the integral role of the phonographic sector. Tschmuck underscores the interconnectedness of music production elements involving music publishers, broadcasting, concert promoters, royalties-collecting societies, and the music instrument industry. Tschmuck traces the evolution from court-dependent musicians to independent composers who capitalized on opportunities in the music publishing industry since the late eighteenth century. The book concludes with an exploration of the transformation triggered by the invention of the phonograph around 1900, integrating the phonographic industry into the broader music industry landscape.

Chapter "New Technology and the Emergence of Jazz" in the same publication (Tschmuck, 2006b), explores the transformative impact of technological innovations on the jazz genre during the critical period from 1920 to 1945. This era marked a significant technological leap with the introduction of electrical recording technology, which greatly enhanced sound quality and facilitated the nuanced recordings necessary for jazz's intricate melodies and complex rhythms. These advancements not only broadened the reach of jazz from its live performance roots to a global audience via records but also played a crucial role in the genre's commercialization and popularization. The chapter details how these technological changes influenced both the production and dissemination of jazz, enabling it to become a staple of the recording industry (Tschmuck, 2006b, 40–60).

Moreover, the chapter delves into the symbiotic relationship between the burgeoning broadcasting industry and the phonographic sector, highlighting how radio emerged as a powerful platform for jazz dissemination. This new medium complemented phonograph records, making jazz accessible to a broader audience and cementing its place in the cultural mainstream (Tschmuck, 2006b, 44–54).

Peter Tschmuck's more recent publication, *The Economics of Music* (Tschmuck, 2021b), delves deeper into the economic intricacies of the modern music industry. This updated edition reflects on the profound shifts brought about by the COVID-19 pandemic, particularly its disruptive impact on live music venues and the consequent adjustments in the industry's revenue models. Tschmuck extends his analysis to include the burgeoning dominance of technology companies and the pivotal role of big data, as well as the evolving influence of collective management organizations in redefining contractual norms and business strategies (Tschmuck, 2021b).

Statistical Data

In the course of this study, statistical data from various authoritative sources has been incorporated to support the research findings and enrich the analysis. Key sources include the *International Federation of the Phonographic Industry's* (hereinafter referred to as IFPI) "Global Music Report 2021–2023," which provides comprehensive insights into the global music industry landscape, including trends, revenues, and market dynamics (IFPI, 2024b). *Statista 2024* offers datasets and analytics on music consumption patterns and digital streaming statistics. Music & Copyright 2021b and *Music & Copyright 2023* contribute additional depth with their focused analyses on intellectual property issues, licensing trends, and the economic impacts of copyright laws on the music sector. These sources collectively form the empirical foundation of this study, ensuring that the conclusions drawn are grounded in robust and up-to-date evidence (Music & Copyright, 2023).

A very useful source was the article "30+ Harmonious Music Industry Statistics" by Abby McCain (McCain, 2023b). The article proves invaluable, as it synthesizes key data from authoritative sources like *Mordor Intelligence*, IFPI, and *Statista* and compiles the music industry research summary after the year 2020. It shows the dominance of streaming in generating industry revenues, with an insightful breakdown of market shares among major streaming services and their payment rates to artists. This detailed aggregation of recent statistics and trends offers a robust quantitative foundation to discuss the evolution and economic dynamics of the music industry, emphasizing the pivotal role of digital platforms in shaping market behavior and artist income (IFPI, 2023b, IFPI, 2024b).

These data sources serve as indispensable tools for this book, offering a comprehensive overview of market trends, revenue streams, and emerging dynamics within the music industry. The statistics taken from these reports provide crucial insights that facilitate a deeper understanding of the industry's trajectory, give a general perspective on the music industry, and enable a more informed discussion of its future directions and challenges.

The Table 1.2 below summarizes the overall use of literature sources by categories.

1.3.2 Semi-Structured Interviews

Semi-structured interviews are a useful method of data collection in social science research, particularly when the research question requires both standardized and open-ended data. The researcher uses a set of standardized questions as a starting point but also allows for more flexibility and open-ended conversation (Tsang, 2022).

The questions are designed to elicit specific information related to the research topic, but the interviewer also follows up on interesting or unexpected responses

Table 1.2 The overview of examined documents (the author)

Categorization of examined documents	
Category 1	Statistical data
Category 2	Literature specialized in the music business and recording industry
Category 3	Popular literature
Category 4	Informal guides published by music industry practitioners
Category 5	Research papers on problematics of the independent music industry
Category 6	The websites of the engaged micro-enterprises
Category 7	Annual reports of the engaged micro-enterprises
Category 8	Small and medium enterprise (hereinafter referred to as SME) categorization laws

with additional questions. This allows the participant to provide more detail and insights while still maintaining some level of standardization in the data collection process. This helps to ensure that all participants are being asked similar questions while still allowing for individual differences and experiences to be explored (ibid.).

Semi-structured interviews can also help to build rapport and trust between the researcher and the participant, as the conversation is less rigid and more open-ended. This can lead to more detailed and nuanced data, as participants may feel more comfortable sharing their experiences and perspectives (ibid.).

1.3.2.1 Interview Process

The interview questions were carefully crafted to elicit in-depth information about the participants' work, ideas, and approaches to running their independent jazz record labels and working as digital distributors. They were designed to encourage participants to share their experiences and perspectives, stimulate discussion, and delve into specific aspects of their label's or distributor's operations.

Each interview lasted approximately one to one and a half hours. This extended duration allowed for a comprehensive exploration of the topics, ensuring that participants had ample time to share their insights and experiences.

The interviews were conducted remotely, typically via video conferencing tools or phone calls. This approach was chosen for its convenience and flexibility, allowing participants to engage from their respective locations. Remote interviews also eliminated geographical constraints and made it easier to include representatives from diverse backgrounds.

To facilitate the interviews with representatives from jazz micro-labels, the author developed a set of 32 questions, categorized into five distinct sections. Additionally, for the interviews with representatives specializing in digital distribution, the author formulated nine questions focused on identifying trends and proposing strategies within the digital music sector. Detailed descriptions of these questionnaires can be found in Sect. 1.3.2.4, titled "Questionnaire for Professionals from the Recording Industry," and Sect. 1.3.2.5, titled "Questionnaire for

Representatives from the Digital Distribution Sector." Both questionnaires are included in the attachments.

The interview process for this research unfolded with a strategic and diverse approach. Employing existing personal connections, the author reached out to label representatives whom they had encountered professionally in the past. This pre-established connection not only made the outreach process smoother but also contributed to the ease with which the interviews were conducted, fostering an environment of openness and friendliness during the conversations. The list of interviewees was curated intentionally to encompass varied territories, historical backgrounds, and label sizes, ensuring a comprehensive perspective.

While scheduling constraints affected two informants, the author proactively sought alternative participants to maintain the diversity and richness of insights. The interviews predominantly unfolded in English, reflecting the global reach of the research. Only one interview was conducted in Czech, with the responses in Slovak language.

After the initial interview, the author engaged in a reflective review of the questions, adapting them for enhanced effectiveness in subsequent interviews. An additional section, inspired by noteworthy highlights from the initial conversation, was incorporated, enriching the scope of the research.

All interviews, conducted between 2021 and 2024, were facilitated through video conference applications Zoom and Google Meet, enabling an exploration of the strategies employed by independent jazz micro-labels during this timeframe. The initial interview was conducted in 2021, which informed the author's approach to subsequent interviews with label representatives throughout 2022 and 2023. Additionally, three interviews with digital distribution professionals were conducted in 2023 and 2024, further enriching the research.

Leveraging the author's professional background, interviews often transcended formal questioning, transforming into affable conversations delving into industry challenges. This informal exchange also facilitated the sharing of practical tips and advice regarding label management, providing valuable insights beyond the structured interview format. All the interviewees agreed that their names should be publicly used while demonstrating the results of this research.

1.3.2.2 Data Transcription and Coding

Transcription

All interviews were recorded and transcribed verbatim to ensure the accuracy and completeness of the data. Transcription was conducted using various transcription software to streamline the process and maintain consistency in the data, as well as proofreading and editing by the author. During the transcriptions, certain quotes were picked for later use in Chap. 3, "Findings."

Coding

A coding process was employed to organize and analyze the data efficiently. The coding categories were developed based on the question areas to capture key themes and concepts for their later application in the related chapters. Additionally, an Excel spreadsheet was utilized for further coding and organization of data, allowing for a more comprehensive overview of answers related to specific chapters or research questions (Ose, 2016b).

1.3.2.3 The Informant Definition

Nine representatives of independent jazz record labels and three representatives of distribution companies were selected as participants in this study. These individuals were chosen to represent a diverse range of experiences, backgrounds, and operational styles within the independent music industry. The participants' insights were considered crucial for gaining a comprehensive understanding of the subject matter.

A semi-structured interview was conducted with a diverse sample of independent jazz micro-labels. Labels were selected based on their establishment years, sizes, and geographic locations to ensure a comprehensive understanding of the industry. The sample included both well-established and emerging labels to capture a range of perspectives and experiences.

In the context of this study, the independence of an informant is a key factor and is defined in detail in a later chapter. Generally, independence for these labels means that they are not under direct contractual obligations with any of the major labels. Major record labels have established alternative distribution platforms to distribute and advertise music from independent labels (Soundcharts Team, 2022b). For the purposes of this study, micro-companies that collaborate with major labels for distribution purposes are still considered independent if they retain 100 percent of the rights to their albums and release them exclusively under their own label's name. However, this study does not regard a micro-company as independent if it licenses albums to one or more major labels, as this implies a relinquishment of control over the production and distribution of their music, and researching their strategies wouldn't be relevant to this research's range of interest.

This study focuses on label representatives from the U.S.A. and European Union (and further EU) and is strategically grounded in their market leadership (Amos, 2023b). The geographical distribution includes the United Kingdom (hereinafter referred to as UK), Czech Republic, Slovakia, Finland, United States of America (hereinafter referred to as U.S.A.), Germany, and Austria.

The temporal landscape of label establishment showcases a blend of long-standing entities and newer entrants. Labels founded before the year 2000 include ACT Music (est. 1992) and Enja Records (est.1971), reflecting a depth of experience and historical context. Those established between 2000 and 2010 encompass Razdaz Recordz (est. 2002), Hevhetia (est. 2002), and Greenleaf Music (est. 2005), contributing perspectives from the transformative early twenty-first century. Labels initiated after 2010, such as Heartcore Records (est. 2016), We Jazz Records (est. 2016), Freifeld Tontraeger (est. 2022), and Ma Records (est. 2020), bring a fresh outlook, navigating the contemporary challenges and opportunities in the evolving music industry.

Overall, in this study, the researcher has opted to examine independent jazz micro-labels with various years of establishment, functioning across diverse geographical regions in the EU and U.S.A. Each label is characterized by an artist roster representing international talent. Despite operating in diverse locations, these labels face similar challenges in effectively disseminating and marketing their musical productions on a global scale.

Kervin M. Dockendorf (DE), Kyle McEvoy (U.S.A.), and Naemi Wetter (DE), all three distinguished for their active roles and extensive expertise in digital distribution, were interviewed alongside representatives of independent jazz micro-labels to elucidate current trends in the digital music landscape. McEvoy, based in upstate New York, is a multi-instrumentalist, producer, and CEO of Sonder House and Only One on the Mountain, bringing a wealth of experience in digital distribution, A&R on streaming, and label management. Dockendorf, the founder and managing director of Germany-based Fangtasia Music, possesses over 9 years of formal industry experience and 17 years as a freelancer, specializing in comprehensive music and video distribution services. As a representative of an independent distributor working under a major label, the author interviewed Naemi Wetter from the German branch of The Orchard, SME's alternative distributor (Table 1.3).

Table 1.3 The overview of informants (the author)

Digital distributors		
The company	**Label representative**	**Based**
Fangtasia music	Kervin M. Dockendorf	DE
Sonder house, the only one on the mountain	Kyle McEvoy	U.S.A.
The orchard	Naemi wetter	DE

Independent jazz micro-labels			
The company	**Label representative**	**Based**	**Founded**
ACT Music	Andreas Brandis	Germany	1992
Enja Records	Werner Aldinger	Germany	1971
Freifeld Tontraeger	Alexander Yannilos	Austria	2015
Greenleaf Music	Dave Douglas	U.S.A.	2005
Heartcore Records	Kurt Rosenwinkel	Germany	2016
Hevhetia	Ján Súdzina	Slovakia	2002
Ma Records	Vojta Drnek	Czech Republic	2020
Razdaz Recordz	Ray Jefford	United Kingdom	2002
We Jazz Records	Matti Nives	Finland	2016

1.3.2.4 Questionnaire for the Professionals from the Recording Industry

The survey was divided into five sections, covering various aspects of the labels: (1) Introduction, (2) Financial aspects, (3) Distribution aspects, (4) Product aspects, and (5) Marketing aspects. The questions were carefully structured to elicit detailed responses, ensuring a comprehensive understanding of each label's unique circumstances.

The first section captures specifics about the label, including its establishment year, product types, and artist development departments. The second section delves into financial aspects, exploring income sources, budget allocation, and funding channels. The third section investigates the labels' relationships with digital distribution and streaming services. The fourth section focuses on product strategies, including the types of products produced and distribution channels used. The fifth section addresses marketing, with a focus on the digital environment. This section also focuses on labels' special projects and community engagement and examines the influence of their strategies on the label's repertoire.

The questionnaire (see Attachment 1) was used as a leading map for the semi-structured interview executed and interpreted by the author of this book. It investigates their primary revenue streams and anticipates future changes in these sources. Questions also explore whether these labels integrate record sales and merchandising with other music industry sectors, such as live concert ticket sales or licensing. Further inquiries address the labels' responses to digitization and streaming, their utilization of available tools within today's music industry, and their strategic adaptations to significant industry changes. Additionally, the questionnaire examines if there exists a common trend in labels' strategic approaches and how these strategies influence their musical repertoire.

1.3.2.5 Questionnaire for Representatives from the Digital Distribution Sector

The research targets key informants from the digital distribution sector, specifically owners and/or managers of companies Kervin M. Dockendorf, Kyle McEvoy, and Naemi Wetter. The goal is to gather qualitative data that focuses on effective income channels, revenue maximization, label-distributor collaborations, strategic planning, and future trends within the niche market of independent jazz labels.

The questionnaire (Attachment 2) comprises nine questions designed to elicit detailed and actionable responses from the informants. Key questions include identifying the most effective income channels in the digital space, strategies for maximizing opportunities within digital distribution, and tools within streaming services that can boost artist visibility. It also explores the common pitfalls in label-distributor collaborations and ways to avoid them. Further questions focus on advice for independent jazz micro-labels, budget allocation for digital marketing, the pros and cons of different distribution companies, and their perspectives on the future of physical sales versus digital royalties for jazz labels.

Sources

Amos, M. (2023b). Which country has the biggest music industry in 2023? RouteNote. https://routenote.com/blog/which-country-has-the-biggest-music-industry-in-2023/

Act Music. 2024. "About ACT." ACT Music Official Website. https://www.actmusic.com/en/About-ACT/ACT-Music

Bartmanski, D., & Woodward, I. (2020b). *Labels: Making independent music*. Bloomsbury Academic.

Dias, J., & Medbøe, H. (2014b). Improvisation in the digital age: New narratives in jazz promotion and dissemination. *First Monday, 19*(10). https://doi.org/10.5210/fm.v19i10.5553

Gray, H. (1983b). *Producing jazz: The experience of an independent record company*. Temple University Press.

Greenwood, C. (2023b). *Spotify profits 2.0: Music marketing and business strategies for the new singles economy*. Chris Greenwood.

Hitters, E., & den Drijver, R. (2017b). The business of DIY. Characteristics, motives and ideologies of micro-independent record labels. *Cadernos de Arte e Antropologia, 6*(1), 17–35. https://doi.org/10.4000/cadernosaa.1192

Hutchison, T. W., Strasser, R., & Hull, G. P. (2011). *The music business and recording industry: Delivering music in the 21st century*. Routledge.

IFPI. (2023b). Engaging with music 2023. IFPI. https://www.ifpi.org/wp-content/uploads/2023/12/IFPI-Engaging-With-Music-2023_full-report.pdf

IFPI. (2024b). Global music report 2024. IFPI. https://ifpi-website-cms.s3.eu-west-2.amazonaws.com/IFPI_GMR_2024_State_of_the_Industry_db92a1c9c1.pdf.

McCain, A. (2023b). 30+ harmonious music industry statistics [2023]: Worth, data, and revenue. Zippia. https://www.zippia.com/advice/music-industry-statistics/

Morgen, B. A. (2022). Optimisation of musical distribution in streaming services: Third-party playlist promotion and algorithmic logics of distribution. In G. Morrow, D. Nordgård, & P. Tschmuck (Eds.), *Rethinking the music business: Music contexts, rights, data, and COVID-19*. Springer International Publishing. https://doi.org/10.1007/978-3-031-09532-0_9

Music & Copyright. (2021b). UMG and SME put the market share squeeze on WMG and the independent sector. Music & Copyright's Blog. https://musicandcopyright.wordpress.com/2021/04/21/umg-and-sme-put-the-market-share-squeeze-on-wmg-and-the-independent-sector/

Music & Copyright. (2023). *Market Share – Music & Copyright's Blog*. Music & Copyright's Blog. https://musicandcopyright.wordpress.com/tag/market-share/

Ose, S. O. (2016b). Using excel and word to structure qualitative data. *Journal of Applied Social Science, 10*(2), 147–162. https://doi.org/10.1177/1936724416664948

Other Records Labels. (2022b). *Record label marketing strategies – 25 practical concepts*. Other Record Labels.

Soundcharts Team. (2022b). A complete guide to music distribution companies. Soundcharts. https://soundcharts.com/blog/music-distribution

Tsang, G. (2022). *A peep at the current state of jazz music through data from Spotify (part 1)*. George Tsang. https://tsanggeorge.medium.com/a-peep-at-the-current-state-of-jazz-music-through-data-from-spotify-part-1-75400069f2dc

Tschmuck, P. (2006b). *Creativity and innovation in the music industry*. Springer.

Tschmuck, P. (2021b). *The economics of music*. Agenda Publishing.

Chapter 2
Basic Terms Definition

Abstract This chapter provides essential context for all topics considered in this book, offering a comprehensive understanding of the recording industry, the strategies employed by micro-enterprises, and the specific challenges faced by independent jazz labels. It traces the evolution of the recording industry, emphasizing how technological advancements and changes in formats have continually reshaped the role of record labels. The concept of independence is explored in relation to the broader music industry, focusing on the opportunities and challenges it presents for small, independent labels in contrast to major companies.

The chapter also examines jazz as a genre, exploring its origins in the late nineteenth and early twentieth centuries, and its integration into the recording industry. It discusses the historical development of jazz labels, their influence on the genre, and the current state of independent jazz labels in the digital age. Finally, the chapter outlines the strategies available to micro-enterprises, including financial, product, distribution, and marketing approaches, highlighting the tools that independent labels can leverage to navigate the evolving music industry.

2.1 The Recording Industry Within the Music Industries Context

The recording industry is one of the three main industries in the world of music business, together with the music licensing industry and live music industry. These three departments are closely related; however, they function in different systems and structures (Wikström, 2014, 10). There are other companies in the music industry, such as makers of music instruments, software, stage equipment, music merchandise, etc. However, while these are important industry sectors, they are traditionally not considered to be integral parts of the industry's core (Wikström, 2014, 10).

M. Drnek Bóková, *Strategies of Micro-Enterprises in the Recording Industry*,
Music Business Research, https://doi.org/10.1007/978-3-031-88439-9_2

According to Tschmuck (2021), the recording industry, music publishing, and the live music sector are closely linked yet follow distinct production, distribution, and consumption logics. Recording companies typically encompass both recording and music publishing branches, relying on publishing copyrights. The concert business not only generates significant revenue for musicians but also aids in selling recorded music, with studies showing these markets are complementary. Music-collecting societies link musicians to industry sectors, administering rights and licensing music use for live performances, broadcasting, digital platforms, and media. The recording industry's adaptation to the digital landscape includes direct licensing to digital providers and media synchronization rights (ibid.).

Furthermore, the recording industry not only leads in setting economic and cultural trends but also plays an important role in determining which genres and artists gain prominence. This influence extends to live music programming and publishing decisions, highlighting the recording industry's critical role in shaping the direction and health of the broader music industries. Tschmuck also discusses the industry's adaptability to consumer preferences and technological changes, setting precedents for other sectors within the music industry to follow (Tschmuck, 2006, 68–70, 94–95).

Before the century break, when the Internet overtook the main role in recorded music consumption, the recording industry was the biggest of the three concerning revenue. Live music traditionally supported record sales, and the licensing revenues were a smaller part of the overall income. At the end of the twentieth century, when the Internet challenged the complete system, the recording industry was the most affected of these three branches. The licensing and the live music industries, on the other hand, gained more power and importance during the last 20 years (Wikström, 2014, 10) with the exception of the COVID pandemic period when the live music industry experienced a 98 percent year-on-year revenue decline in Q2 2020, driven by global concert shutdowns (Stone, 2020).

Unlike music publishing, the recording industry faced substantial challenges from digitization. According to the IFPI, the global sound recording market shrank by 46.6 percent between 1998 and 2014 but later rebounded thanks to the surge in music streaming (Sect. 2.2.1: The Current State of the Recording Industry). To navigate the digital music landscape, record companies had to overhaul their business models, redefining essential functions such as artist and repertoire (A&R), production, and marketing (Tschmuck, 2021, 89).

2.2 Recording Industry

The history of the recording industry goes back to the end of the nineteenth century, which was marked by Edison's invention of the phonograph in 1877. In the following decade, Emil Berliner's first gramophone appeared on the market. Later technological developments introduced music on vinyl, the gradual improvement that led to the Long Play (hereinafter referred to as LP) format, which had its heyday in the 1970s and 1980s (Kees, 1998, 458).

Philips introduced the compact cassette in 1963. This new format was designed for ease of use in both playback and recording, which made it extremely popular for personal use and portable music players. Despite initial resistance from major record labels, the compact cassette eventually found a significant market, particularly with the introduction of the Dolby noise reduction system in 1966, which improved playback quality. The compact cassette became especially dominant in regions with lower purchasing power, such as parts of Asia and Africa, due to its affordability and ease of mass reproduction, often outside the control of major labels (Tschmuck, 2006, 150).

The introduction of the Compact Disc (hereinafter referred to as CD) in the early 1980s and its boom in 1987–1988 significantly transformed the music distribution and consumption landscape. The recording industry underwent substantial structural changes. Tschmuck outlines how these technological advancements facilitated the expansion of music catalogs and the reach of record labels, setting the stage for subsequent consolidations (ibid., 152).

As the industry capitalized on the technological innovations that CDs brought, major record labels began to merge and acquire smaller entities to strengthen their market positions and maximize profits. The consolidation was driven by the necessity to manage extensive music catalogs more effectively and respond to the rapid digitalization of music. This phase of consolidation reflected the labels' strategies to maintain control over the burgeoning digital music market and adapt to the global shifts in music consumption patterns (ibid.).

The recording industry saw major consolidation from the 1960s into the twenty-first century, particularly with the acquisition of smaller companies by major record labels. By 1999, the recording music industry was controlled by the so-called "Big Five"—Warner Music Group (hereinafter referred to as WMG), EMI, Sony Music Entertainment (hereinafter referred to as SME), BMG, and Universal Music Group (hereinafter referred to as UMG)—whose oligopoly accounted for 70–80 percent of global music sales (Music & Copyright, 2021). In 2004, the joint venture of Sony and BMG created the "Big Four," and in 2014, American and European regulators approved the UMG and SME's takeover of EMI, which resulted with the creation of "Big Three"[1] (Witt, 2015).

The boom in CD sales was halted at the turn of the century with the advent of Napster (1999) and other peer-to-peer services (hereinafter referred to as P2P). These piracy platforms offered music for free, disrupting the conventional economics of the recording industry. The efforts to replicate the market advantages of the streaming music model were largely unsuccessful until 2008 when Spotify's streaming model stemmed the tidal waves of pirated music and created a new perspective for renewed growth (The Intellectual Property Office, 2019, 29).

Today, the recording industry seeks new opportunities to multiply its profits and adapt to new ways of music consumption that change according to technological

---

[1] According to Music & Copyright, the three largest record labels—Universal Music Group (32 percent market share), Sony Music Entertainment (20 percent), and Warner Music Group (16 percent)—hold a 68 percent share of the music recording market in 2019.

development and new trends in digitization (Arditi, 2021, 156). Despite these trends, the recent vinyl resurgence reflects a broader cultural trend of seeking tangible, high-quality music experiences, highlighting the enduring appeal of physical media in an increasingly digitized world (Palm, 2017).

2.2.1 The Current State of the Recording Industry

> "*Given that throughout the twentieth century jazz was present in (and indeed spearheaded) many of the technological revolutions in the music industry, it now seems rather to lag, and even resist, change.*" (Dias & Medbøe, 2014, 12)

Streaming has had an increasingly important position in the music market since 2004. In 2023, the global music industry experienced its ninth successive year of revenue growth, according to the IFPI's Global Music Report, with total recorded music revenues reaching an unprecedented $28.6 billion (Fig. 2.1). This growth was primarily driven by streaming services (Fig. 2.2), which contributed $19.3 billion, alongside a resurgence in physical music sales that accumulated $5.1 billion, bolstered by increased CD sales and the sustained popularity of vinyl (Fig. 2.1). This rebound marks a significant turnaround from 2014 when the industry faced a 20-year revenue low of $13.0 billion, a stark contrast to the peak of the CD era. Initially hesitant to transition to digital formats, the industry has now fully embraced streaming, which now constitutes 67 percent of total music revenues. By the end of 2023, streaming platforms boasted 667 million paid subscriptions, indicating a robust adoption that far surpasses the peak of digital downloads. This transition underscores a critical recovery phase for the industry, which had previously suffered a devastating decline due to the rise of MP3 and file-sharing technologies, erasing $14 billion in annual revenue from physical sales. The revival of the music industry's fortunes can be largely attributed to the widespread adoption and integration of music streaming services (Richter, 2024).

Although sales of physical music in the jazz industry are still reflected (Sect. 2.6.1: Jazz Recording Industry) and have grown in the last 3 years (Fig. 2.1), streaming's leadership in the global industry revenue has grown exponentially (Fig. 2.2). Considering the trends in the global music industry, it is essential for jazz labels to focus on building the customer community and young listeners more intensively within streaming services while looking for alternatives for additional revenue to sustain their organization and create financial success (Dias & Medbøe, 2014).

In the same study, "Improvisation in the Digital Age: New Narratives in Jazz Promotion and Dissemination" (ibid.), authors examine how jazz's diminished presence in mainstream media has driven its artists to seek new ways to connect with audiences and build communities. Traditional jazz promoters and critics often cling to outdated methods of presentation that resonate with the genre's historical image. Despite the potential of the online jazz community, it often gets overshadowed by the vast array of digital content available. The jazz world finds itself at a crossroads, balancing traditional, in-person interactions with the expansive, ever-changing

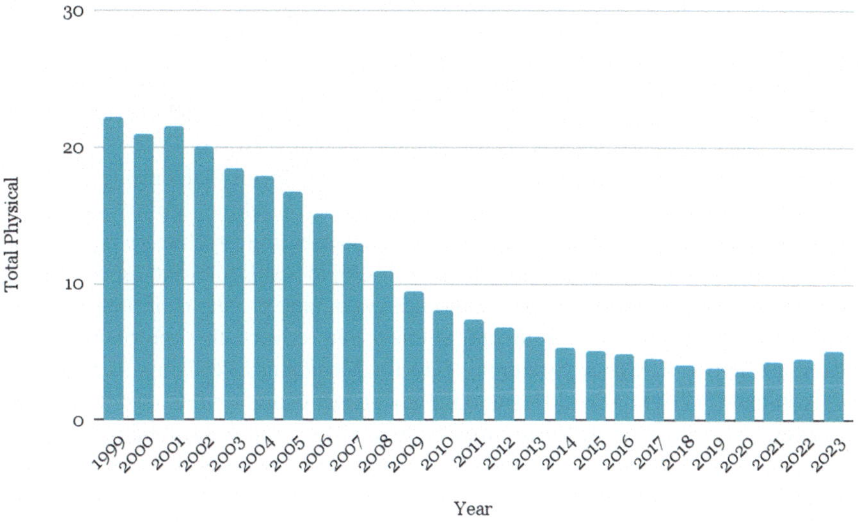

Fig. 2.1 Global recorded music industry revenues from physical format 1999–2023 (US$ billions) (IFPI, 2024, processed by the author)

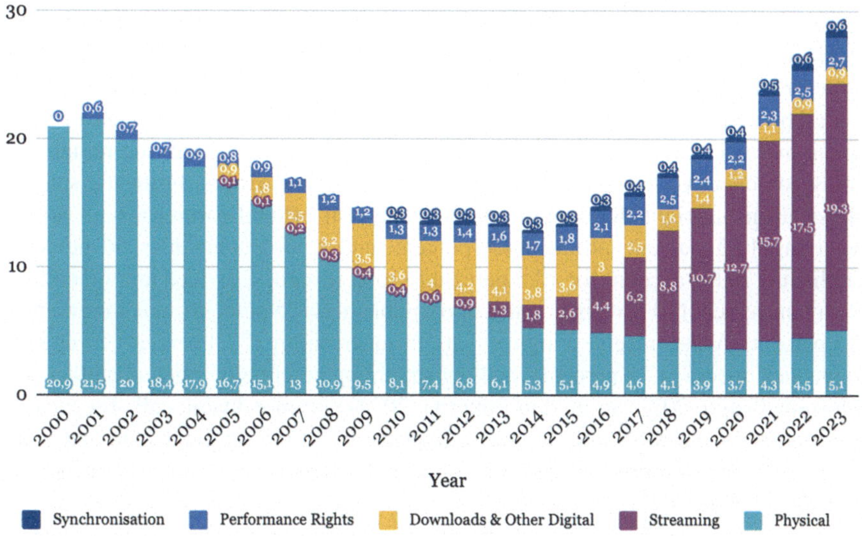

Fig. 2.2 Global recorded music industry revenues 1999–2023 (US$ billions) (IFPI, 2024, processed by the author)

digital landscape. This tension stems from jazz's deep-rooted adherence to tradition, making it challenging to fully embrace new technologies for creation and distribution. Consequently, while the jazz industry shows resistance to cultural and technological evolution, musicians are tasked with reinventing their approaches to thrive in the digital era, often working against entrenched industry norms (ibid.).

The general revenue in the music industry is increasing, mostly due to the existence of streaming services. It is up to the micro-enterprises to find the best way to take advantage of the rising aspects of the industry (IFPI, 2024).

In the field of streaming music, there are several platforms that, despite the positive impact on the economy of the music industry as a whole, are the subject of controversial complaints due to the system of redistributing royalties to representative organizations and, by extension, artists. This topic is still relevant, especially for the "streamshare" economic policy and other systematic problems of the royalties' distribution. One of the significant studies that covers this problematics is Hesmondhalgh's "Is Music Streaming Bad for Musicians? Problems of Evidence and Argument" (2021). David Hesmondhalgh's paper examines the impact of music streaming services (hereinafter referred to as MSS) on musicians, highlighting the persistent inequalities in income distribution despite the increased ability for more musicians to earn from recorded music. Hesmondhalgh argues that criticisms often focus too narrowly on "per-stream" rates without considering the broader systemic context, including the complexity of revenue distribution influenced by contracts and overall MSS income. The debate over pro-rata versus user-centric payment models is significant, with the latter potentially offering fairer revenue shares to niche artists compared to the current system favoring popular ones (Hesmondhalgh, 2021). Historically, musicians have received low percentages from record sales, and the current streaming model might offer better outcomes for some. According to research cited by Pokorná (2024, pp. 43–46), artists receive 22.4 percent of total streaming revenues, while record labels receive 42.4 percent, with the remainder going to collective management organizations and songwriters. From the sale of physical media, rights holders receive 87.5 percent of total earnings, with artists receiving 17.5 percent, producers 4 percent, and record companies 66 percent. Publishing rights account for 12.5 percent of total revenues, divided among collective management (10 percent commission), publishers (25 percent), and songwriters (75 percent). Artists receive a higher share from streaming (22.4 percent) compared to physical media (17.5 percent), making streaming potentially more advantageous (Hesmondhalgh, 2021, as cited in Pokorná, 2024). Hesmondhalgh calls for greater transparency from MSS and the music industry to inform public debate and consider necessary reforms to improve fairness and equity in revenue distribution (Hesmondhalgh, 2021).

Despite the controversy, the number of users of these services is increasing rapidly (Fig. 2.3) and is becoming a major source of profits for the music industry. Their numerous activities, which include special services not only for users but also for creators, expand their customer base and music library every year (IFPI, 2023). Forecasts promise economic growth in the music market, which will be primarily linked to the growth of the streaming giant Spotify and its competitors such as Amazon.com, Inc., Apple, Inc., Google, Inc., Tencent Music Entertainment Group (Tencent Holdings Ltd.), SoundCloud Ltd., Sirius XM Holdings, Inc. (Pandora

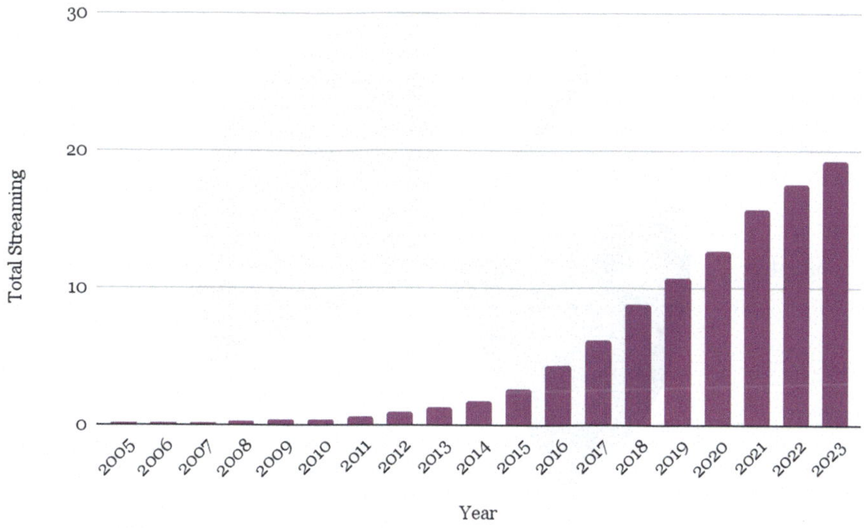

Fig. 2.3 Global recorded music industry revenues from streaming 1999–2023 (US$ billions) (IFPI, 2024, processed by the author)

Media, Inc.), iHeartMedia, Inc. (Thomas H. Lee Partners), Deezer S.A. (Access Industries Holdings LLC) and Aspiro AB (Tidal) (Schafer, 2021).

Figure 2.4 illustrates the share of the leading streaming services in the global market. Spotify continues to dominate the global music streaming market with a commanding 31.7 percent share, more than double that of its nearest competitor, Tencent Music, at 14.4 percent. Apple Music and Amazon follow closely, capturing 12.6 percent and 11.1 percent of the market, respectively, showing a strong presence among tech giants. YouTube Music's 9.7 percent share highlights its significant, albeit smaller, role in the industry. NetEase and Yandex, with 6.7 percent and 3.4 percent, respectively, reflect regional strengths, while Deezer's 1.3 percent indicates a niche user base. The remaining 9.7 percent under "Other" suggests a fragmented market with numerous smaller players (MIDiA Research, 2024).

Following the extensive advancements in streaming services, artificial intelligence (hereinafter referred to as AI) has begun to play a pivotal role in transforming the music industry. AI technologies automate various aspects of music creation, such as content generation, vocal synthesis, and track separation. This has significantly enhanced music production and restoration capabilities, exemplified by isolating John Lennon's voice for The Beatles' song "Now And Then." Beyond these applications, AI algorithms analyze data to predict music trends and listener preferences, enhancing personalized recommendations on streaming platforms. AI also automates mixing and mastering processes, and involves in music composition by generating melodies and harmonies. AI plays a role in detecting copyright infringements and managing digital rights, fostering a secure environment for creators. However, these advancements raise ethical dilemmas, including the unauthorized use of artists' voices and the influx of AI-generated content on streaming platforms.

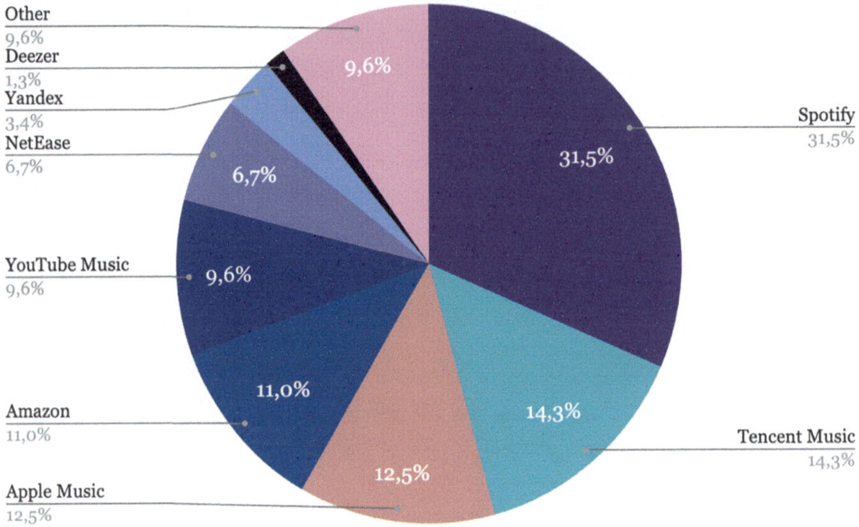

Fig. 2.4 Share of music streaming subscribers worldwide in the third quarter of 2023 by a company (MIDiA Research, 2024, processed by the author)

Such developments prompt critical discussions about the future of creativity and the evolving role of human artists in the industry. Moreover, it was revealed in May 2023 that up to 10 percent of all music streamed on Spotify might be "fake music," comprising 31-second AI-generated loops created to divert revenue streams (Carter, 2024).

Balancing technological innovation with artistic integrity remains a central concern as the industry continues to evolve (Semancik, 2024).

2.3 Micro-Enterprises

According to the European Commission, micro-enterprises are defined as businesses that employ fewer than ten people and have an annual turnover or balance sheet total of no more than 2 million euros. These small businesses are considered the backbone of the European economy, accounting for the majority of all businesses and providing essential goods and services to local communities (European Commission, 2020).

Micro-enterprises are often owner-operated and operate on a local or regional scale. They are diverse in nature, ranging from independent contractors and sole traders to small family businesses and artisanal producers. They can be found in a wide range of sectors, including agriculture, retail, manufacturing, services, and artistic organizations (ibid.).

Despite their small size, micro-enterprises face many of the same challenges as larger businesses, including market competition, regulatory compliance, and access to financing. However, they also benefit from greater flexibility, agility, and a strong sense of community (Catalano, 2023).

The European Commission recognizes the important role that micro-enterprises play in creating jobs, promoting innovation, and driving economic growth. As such, it provides a range of support measures and initiatives to help these businesses thrive and succeed in an ever-changing and competitive market. Small and medium enterprises (hereinafter referred to as SME) represent 99 percent of all businesses in the European Union (hereinafter referred to as the EU) and are a fundamental component of its economy. According to 2012 statistics, these types of businesses provided almost 90 million jobs and thus generated up to two-thirds of all jobs in the EU. In addition, SMEs stimulate entrepreneurship and innovation, thus supporting European competitiveness, economic growth, and employment (European Commission, 2020).

Although a different model is employed in the U.S.A., the declared objectives and fundamental principles are the same. A microenterprise, also known as a microbusiness, is the most common type of business and is classified as a company with 1–9 employees by the Small Business Administration (Office Of Advocacy, 2023). There might be other conditions for different states of the U.S.A. For example in the state of Vermont, the Micro Business is defined as a business under five employees (Micro Business Development Program | Department for Children and Families, 2023).

Enterprises that fall under this category have annual sales and asset values of under $250,000. As a startup, these microenterprises often require less than $35,000 in loan capital and lack access to traditional commercial banking. Entrepreneurship, which acknowledges that people have the right to use their unique abilities, ingenuity, and hard effort to improve their lives, is the cornerstone of microenterprises in the United States (Small Business Facts: The Role of Microbusiness Employers in the Economy 2023).

The study defines micro-enterprises based on the criteria set by the European Commission, specifically focusing on businesses with fewer than ten employees.

This method aligns closely with similar definitions used in the United States, ensuring uniformity in the characterization of micro-enterprises across both regions. This focus allows for a precise and consistent framework for identifying informants from this business segment within the EU context for the study.

Although the EU Commission's definition also includes considerations of annual turnover or balance sheet total not exceeding 2 million euros, this research solely utilizes the number of employees as the defining characteristic. The author chose not to inquire about the companies' annual income to avoid delving into their financial situations, as many of these businesses are intertwined with other enterprises, operate on a voluntary basis, or are closely linked to the personal income of the owners.

2.4 Record Label

The authors of the dictionary *Music Business Handbook* describe a record label as "*a company that coordinates the production, manufacture, distribution, marketing, and promotion of audio and video recordings, maintains their legal protection, and negotiates contracts with artists and their management. At the same time, the record label builds a brand through marketing activities related to audio and audiovisual recordings*" (Macy et al., 2016, 7). In summary, a record label serves as a comprehensive entity that manages various aspects of the music business, from the creation of recordings to their distribution and promotion. The label's role extends beyond the purely creative aspects, encompassing legal, business, and marketing functions to ensure the success of the artists and the label itself in the competitive music industry (Macy et al., 2016, 7).

As recently as a decade ago, signing with a major record label might have been the ultimate dream for many aspiring artists. However, the music industry landscape has shifted significantly, and the once-dominant major labels have seen a decline in their prestige and influence. Smaller labels and independent artists are now gaining prominence, raising questions about the true value of a record label in today's music business (Paine, 2022).

The traditional role of major labels encompassed artist development, distribution, and marketing. In the past, these functions were crucial for artists to succeed, especially for those lacking industry connections or significant financial resources. However, the game has changed. Smaller teams and interconnected networks are no longer absolute necessities, and bold managers are identified as a significant threat to record labels. With the rise of social media, artists and managers can now handle the creative and community management aspects of music independently (Kordestani, 2022).

Nevertheless, record labels still play a vital role in artist development, focusing on individual growth, profitability, and data-driven results. They act as patrons of the arts, offering guidance to musicians in finding their niche and navigating the complexities of the industry. Despite the changing dynamics, record labels, both big and small, continue to serve as profit-seeking patrons in the evolving music industry (ibid.).

According to Macy et al., the record label can and should deliver the influence of radio airplay, social media, imaging, and word of mouth. "*Ideally, a label should be the branding agent, the megaphone, and the central intelligence agency on behalf of the artist and recording to create awareness of not only the music but that artist who created it*" (Macy et al., 2016, 5). Today's business model of record labels basically consists of the search for new talents and the pursuit of their so-called "branding." Labels' financial income is no longer solely dependent on the sale of physical or digital media—in order to succeed, they must use both the assets of the audio recording and the reputation of the artist to maximize the potential income of the organization (Macy et al., 2016, 7).

2.5 Independent Record Labels

To be independent, according to the Cambridge Dictionary, means not to be influenced or controlled by other people, events, or things and not accept help or financial support from others (Cambridge Dictionary, 2024); in the context of the music business, being independent means not being part of one of the big companies (Hayes, 2020). Independent record labels, also known as indie record labels or simply "indies," are music companies that are not owned or operated by major corporations or conglomerates. Today, the music industry's leading organizations are reduced to "Big Three"—UMG, WMG, and SME (Hayes, 2020).

According to the World Independent Report (Wintrends, 2022), a notable characteristic of this sector is its constant renewal, with new companies consistently emerging to navigate the evolving landscape. These independent music companies engage with artists on an exclusive and licensed basis, providing a diverse array of deals within the marketplace. Despite the challenges posed by the pandemic, the sector has demonstrated its commitment to creativity by continuing to release new records, with only a minority of releases being preexisting recordings (Worldwide Independent Network, 2022).

In terms of the organizational structure, independent music companies are predominantly micro, small, or medium-sized enterprises, with approximately two-thirds of these companies having five or fewer employees. Although these companies may have relatively few direct employees, they play a significant role in generating indirect employment, thereby contributing substantially to the economies of their respective countries. This underscores the far-reaching impact and importance of the independent music sector beyond its immediate workforce (Worldwide Independent Network, 2022).

Unlike major labels, which often have significant financial and marketing resources, independent labels are typically smaller and more focused on developing unique or niche artists and genres. They are often started by music enthusiasts or musicians themselves, who have a passion for a particular taste, style, or scene and want to support and promote emerging talent within that community (Hitters & den Drijver, 2017, 18). An example is Ma Records in Prague, which started its activity based on a lack of a platform for young musicians to perform and record contemporary and experimental jazz music. Some labels may also be established by business professionals who see a gap in the market or a potential for growth in a particular genre or region. As an instance, we can name an independent record label, Hevhetia, based in Slovakia, that was founded by Jan Súdzina, who recognized the potential of a local jazz scene and aimed to support its artists.

While independent record labels may have more limited resources than major labels, they often offer artists more creative control, flexibility, and autonomy in their artistic direction and business decisions. They may also have closer relationships with their artists, providing them with more personalized support and guidance (Crane, 1976). Independent labels can operate on a local, regional, or international level (Bell & Johansson, 2016), and they can also have a particular aesthetic or ethos that sets them apart from major labels, such as a commitment to supporting socially conscious or politically engaged artists (Hitters & den Drijver, 2017). This type of record label can be represented by Heartcore Records, which thrives to support the music education of unprivileged children in its annual project "Heartcore for the World."[2]

In recent years, independent record labels have gained greater prominence and influence in the music industry, thanks in part to the rise of digital distribution and social media. Many labels of this kind have been able to develop large, dedicated fan bases around the world, and some have even achieved mainstream success and critical acclaim (Music & Copyright, 2021). An example of a successful indie label is XL Recordings, which, despite the seemingly contradictory notion of being "the biggest indie record label," is widely recognized as a top contender in the industry. Founded in 1989 as a dance-focused subsidiary of the UK-based Beggars Group, XL Recordings experienced remarkable and unpredictable growth, eventually transforming into a multi-genre independent powerhouse (KEF, 2024). Other independent companies that are economically relevant are Believe/naïve in France, Edel/Kontor and MCP in Germany, Nippon Columbia in Japan, and PIAS in the UK. In the U.S.A., we can name Concord Records, Big Machine, Epitaph Records, or Curb (Tschmuck, 2021, 118).

Major record labels have created alternative distribution platforms to distribute and advertise the music of independent labels (Soundcharts Team, 2022). For the sake of future chapters in this book, micro-companies that collaborate with major labels for distribution will be regarded as independent if they own 100 percent of the rights to their albums and release them solely under their own name. However, this study will not consider a micro-company independent if it licenses albums to one or more major labels.

2.5.1 The Rise of Independents in the Twentieth Century

> "*Independent music publishers have long dominated music publishing and continue to compete well with the majors for major artists' attention.*" (Resnikoff, 2018)

Many scholars and theorists have commented on the commodification of music production in the twentieth century. Technological development has had a profound impact on music commodification, or the transformation of music into a product that can be bought and sold in the marketplace (Savage, 2022).

Music commercialization has become more accessible due to changes in recording, production, distribution, marketing, and promotion technologies. The development of recording technology, from vinyl records to CDs to digital downloads and

[2]This project is a series of charitable initiatives providing musical workshops and recording sessions for disadvantaged youth globally, with proceeds from digital song downloads funding musical equipment for the children (heartcore-records.com/pages/heartcore-for-the-world).

streaming, has enabled music to be commodified in a variety of formats. It has also made music more accessible to consumers, as they can now purchase music in physical or digital formats (Taylor, 2015).

Advances in production technology, such as digital audio workstations and software synthesizers, have made it easier and more affordable for musicians to produce high-quality recordings. This has opened up the market to independent artists and small record labels, who may not have had the resources to produce music in the past. The development of recording technology has given many creators the freedom to create music essentially from home on a low budget (Walzer, 2017).

In the same era, the music market began to offer the possibility of digital distribution, from which the emergence of distribution aggregators made a democratic environment for the distribution of digital music albums. The Internet and digital distribution platforms have revolutionized how music is distributed and consumed. Artists can now distribute their music directly to consumers through online platforms and digital aggregators, bypassing traditional record labels and distribution channels (Paul, 2019). The ease of digital reproduction and distribution has also led to challenges in protecting copyright and intellectual property. Piracy and illegal downloading have become major challenges for the music industry, leading to changes in copyright law and the development of new technologies to protect digital content. Economic competition in the recording industry has shifted to the environment of streaming services (Priest, 2021, 1).

Social media platforms and digital advertising have also given artists new ways to market and promote their music. Artists can use targeted advertising on social media such as Facebook, Instagram, TikTok, Twitter, YouTube, or Twitch to reach specific audiences, and they can use social media to engage with fans, build a following, or collect and analyze data (Nwagwu & Akintoye, 2023).

Bartmanski and Woodward (2020) talk about another generation of independent music labels that are entering the market together with the industry developments: "*The emblematic result of this trend towards 'DIY' in the music industry has been the proliferation of small and micro music labels that can give access to more creators to enter the market of recorded music. (…) In an important sense, this changing historical context of the music industry was one important space for opening up the growth of another generation of independent music labels*" (Bartmanski & Woodward, 2020, 63).

The phenomenon is visible in the statistical data for the last decade (Fig. 2.5). In 2010, the share of major labels in the world music market was 76.8 percent (digital and physical albums). UMG had the largest share, followed by SME, then WMG, and the smallest of the four dominant labels, EMI Music, which was bought out by UMG in 2011, increasing UMG's share by 10 percent. The remaining 23.2 percent belonged to independent publishers (Anderton et al., 2013, 27).

The statistics from 2019 and 2020 show that the positions of the major labels did not change, but the share of independent music labels increased significantly (Table 2.1). Since 2010, their world market share has increased by 8.4 percent (Music & Copyright, 2021; Music & Copyright, 2023).

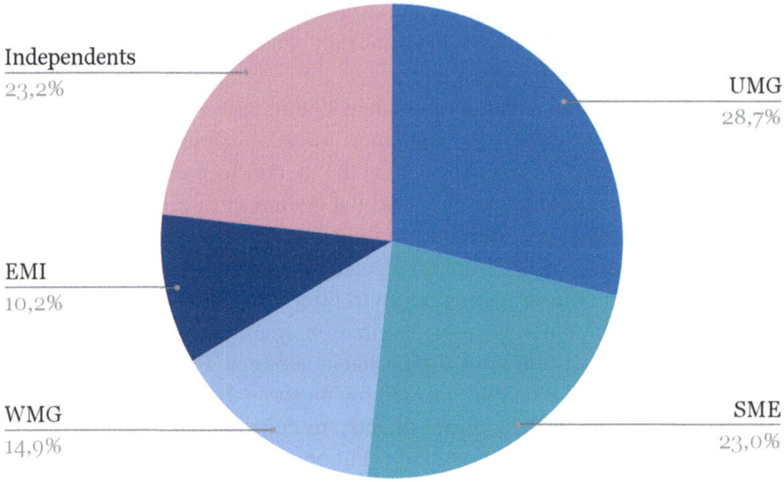

Fig. 2.5 Global recorded music industry market shares 2010 (Informa Telecoms and Media 2011, processed by the author)

Table 2.1 Record companies' physical and digital revenue market shares, 2019 and 2020 (Music & Copyright, 2021, processed by the author)

	Physical		Digital		Physical/Digital	
Percent	2019	2020	2019	2020	2019	2020
UMG	25.8	25.8	33.8	34.1	31.8	32.1
SME	18.3	21.3	20.2	20.5	19.8	20.6
WMG	11.7	10.5	17.9	17.6	16.4	15.6
Independents	44.2	42.4	28.1	27.9	32	31.4

Note: Totals may not add up to 100 percent due to rounding

One of the three major labels, WMG, saw (between 2019 and 2020) a decline in the physical and digital sectors. Furthermore, the gap between the share of physical and digital sales has widened. WMG's physical share fell from 11.7 percent to 10.5 percent, while its digital share saw a more modest decline from 17.9 percent to 17.6 percent.

Although the physical share of independent companies remained high in 2020 (42.4 percent), it decreased from 44.2 percent the previous year. The share of digital distribution also fell from 28.1 percent to 27.9 percent in 2020. The results meant that the combined share of physical and digital revenue for independents fell from 31.9 percent to 31.6 percent, putting them just behind leading major label UMG (Music & Copyright, 2021).

The figures slightly changed and the market share of independent labels decreased to 29.5 percent in 2021 and grew to 30 percent in 2022 considering both digital and

Table 2.2 Record companies' physical/digital revenue market shares, 2021 and 2022 (Music & Copyright, 2023, processed by the author)

	Physical		Digital		Physical/Digital	
Percent	2021	2022	2021	2022	2021	2022
UMG	26.8	27.6	33.3	33	32	31.9
SME	18.5	17.7	22.6	23.2	21.7	22.1
WMG	11.4	10.9	18.2	17.2	16.7	16
Independents	43.2	43.7	25.9	26.5	29.5	30

Note: Totals may not add up to 100 percent due to rounding

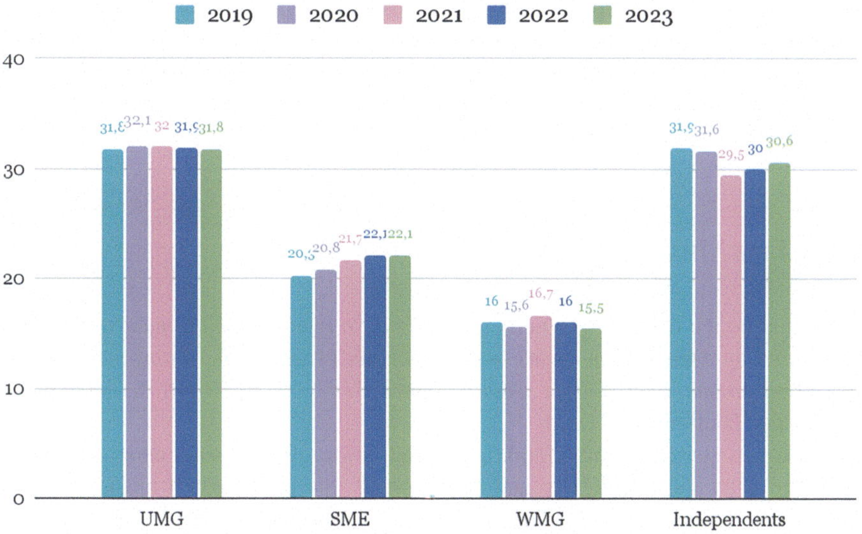

Fig. 2.6 Record companies' physical/digital revenue market share worldwide, 2019–2023 (Music & Copyright, 2021; Music & Copyright, 2023, Statista 2024, processed by the author)

physical format (Table 2.2). If only physical sales are being considered, the independent sector grew from 42.4 percent in 2020 to 43.7 percent in 2022 (Music & Copyright, 2023).

Figure 2.6, illustrating record companies' physical and digital revenue market shares from 2019 to 2023, shows notable trends and shifts in the music industry. UMG consistently held the largest share across both physical and digital formats, with a slight increase in digital market share from 31.8 percent in 2019 to 32.1 percent in 2020. SME experienced minor growth from 20.3 percent in 2019 to 20.8 percent in 2020. WMG, however, saw a decline in both sectors, with its market share dropping from 16 percent to 15.6 percent. Independent labels showed a high physical market share at 31.9 percent in 2019, which slightly decreased to 31.6 percent in 2020 and to 29.5 percent in 2021, but they remained strong and maintained a significant presence, with their overall market share fluctuating and reaching 30 percent in 2022, reflecting the dynamic and competitive nature of the industry. In 2023, UMG held 31.8 percent, SME increased to 22.1 percent, WMG slightly decreased to 15.5 percent, and independents accounted for 30.6 percent of the market share, underscoring ongoing shifts and competition in the music market (Music & Copyright, 2021; Music & Copyright, 2023; Statista 2024).

The proliferation of digital distribution aggregators has democratized music distribution, allowing artists to bypass traditional labels and reach consumers directly. Independent labels have also leveraged new technologies, such as social media and digital advertising, to effectively market and promote their music, engaging directly with fans and building strong followings. Additionally, the COVID-19 pandemic underscored the resilience of independent labels, which quickly adapted to online sales and marketing strategies. The revival of physical formats, particularly vinyl records, has further bolstered independent labels by providing a robust additional revenue stream (Carter, 2024).

2.6 Jazz Music

According to the Cambridge Dictionary, jazz is "*a type of modern music originally developed by African-Americans, with a rhythm in which the strong notes often come before the beat and is usually improvised*" ("jazz | English meaning—Cambridge Dictionary", 2023).

Though a starting point, Cambridge's definition offers a somewhat simplified perspective on the complexity and evolution of this multifaceted musical genre. Christopher Meeder's book, "*Jazz: The Basics*," provides valuable insights into the intricate history of jazz, challenging the notion that its evolution can be depicted as a straightforward line. Meeder emphasizes that the graphic representation of jazz history is more akin to a complex accumulation of parallel lines, reflecting the additive nature of stylistic changes in the arts. Meeder argues that jazz sub-styles experienced fragmentation after the initial era of Bebop musicians, emphasizing individuality and personal style; the coexistence of various jazz styles during different periods was the norm. The Original Dixieland Jass Band's release of what is conventionally considered the first jazz recording already stirred controversy among Midwestern jazz musicians and popular songwriters. Simultaneously, on the East Coast, the evolution of stride piano by pianists and proto-swing dance bands took diverse directions (Meeder, 2012, XIII).

While rooted in African-American musical traditions, jazz has transcended cultural boundaries, incorporating influences from various global sources. The emphasis on improvisation is pertinent, but it is essential to acknowledge that not all jazz is entirely improvised; structured elements also play a crucial role. Additionally, the rhythmic complexity of jazz extends beyond the placement of strong notes, involving intricate time signatures, polyrhythms, and syncopation. Furthermore, the global impact of jazz has contributed to its dynamic and ever-evolving nature, with different regions and cultures influencing and being influenced by this genre. In light of these considerations, a more nuanced and comprehensive understanding of jazz is necessary to appreciate its rich history and diverse expressions within the context of a global musical landscape (Monson et al., 2019).

> "*Jazz is a complex, highly blended, sometimes contradictory music and, indeed, since its inception, it has been hotly debated exactly what forms or styles constitute this music. Is it music theory or a technique that is applied to music? Is it one music or several loosely grouped forms of music that deal with improvisation? Its roots are African and European, classical and popular, dance music and art music. It has been called both cool and hot, earthy and avant-garde, intellectual and primitive.*" (Monson et al., 2019, 7)

In the 1920s, the phenomena of jazz transformed from purely Afro-American music to a "*word for style and attitude, newness, ultramodernity*" (Meltzer, 1993, 74). For over one hundred years, the newness and originality remain the driving forces for jazz artists on the contemporary jazz scene, while other significant stages of jazz music's development are being preserved, quoted, imitated, and put in various contexts with other genres. "*Jazz musicians still beg, borrow, and steal, only now they do it on a global basis. (…) Even in an age in which most music has gone virtual, abandoning the world at hand and descending into the realm of bits and bytes, jazz still rejoices in hand-made (and mouth-made) sound. When you think about it, we really aren't all that far from the music's roots back in New Orleans. We've just added more ingredients to the gumbo*" (Gioia, 2017, 76–77).

The jazz genre today is a complex term to define, and it is unclear where its future lies as it grew and traveled in many different directions and broke into the language of many kinds of current music. "*Whether its (jazz's) future lies as a high-culture, transnational, privileged form of taste and practice or in a new synthesis joining jazz artistry with global hip hop and the popular is an open question. In either case, jazz today is a form of cosmopolitanism. But perhaps that was always what it was striving to be.*" As New York Times jazz critic Ben Ratliff put it: "*There is no American popular music so well miscegenated as jazz*" (Monson et al., 2019, 9).

2.6.1 Jazz Recording Industry

Although jazz is inherently a live art form, our understanding of its history primarily stems from recordings. This development closely paralleled recording technology, with the initial jazz recordings coinciding with the availability of affordable phonographs. As studio technology advanced and new formats emerged, they promptly and significantly influenced how jazz musicians approached their craft (Meeder, 2012, XIII).

While jazz music transcends geographical boundaries and language barriers, fostering a worldwide community of enthusiasts who appreciate its cosmopolitan nature, it remains a niche genre represented by a relatively small number of fans. In contrast to other mainstream genres, its popularity, as evidenced by Media Rating

Council[3] (MRC) data, often ranks considerably lower in the U.S.A. (Fig. 2.7, MRC, 2021, 53).

The study "Youth Music Preferences as Music Education Issues" offers insights into jazz music preferences among various respondent groups across the Czech Republic and other European Union countries. The research revealed that jazz, especially free jazz, received relatively low preference ratings, with only 8.23 percent of Czech respondents having a positive attitude towards free jazz, while traditional jazz fared better with a 90.32 percent positive rating. Furthermore, those with higher levels of music education exhibited more positive attitudes towards jazz, indicating that education enhances the appreciation of more complex music forms. However, overall preferences still leaned towards more accessible mainstream genres, underscoring the challenges jazz faces in broadening its appeal among younger audiences (Rodičová, 2015, 67–77).

According to a 2009 research by Radim Bačuvčík on the Czech Republic's population, men prefer jazz and blues more than women, who lean towards genres like folk, wind music, pop, melodic rock, or classical music. Jazz and blues have a strong following among middle-aged individuals, particularly those in the 30–39 and 50–59 age brackets. Higher education levels correlate with a greater preference for jazz and blues, with many fans holding university degrees or professional music education. The genre is listened to daily by 3.4 percent of respondents, several times a week by 9.4 percent, and several times a month by 13.9 percent, indicating moderate but consistent engagement. Jazz and blues fans are frequent concert attendees and are willing to purchase music, showing a significant investment in their preferred genre. Unlike pop or dance music, jazz, and blues are less likely to be used as

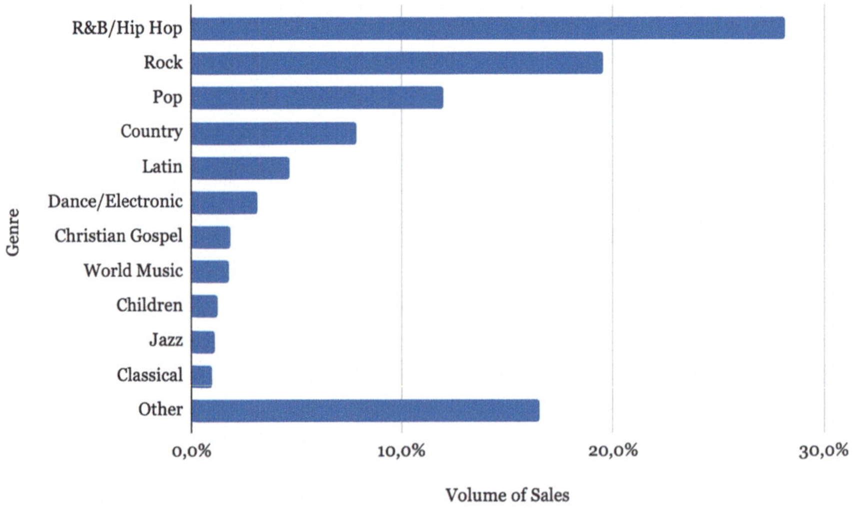

Fig. 2.7 U.S. music genre popularity by sales in 2020 (MRC, 2021, 53, processed by the author)

[3] Formerly Nielsen Soundscan.

background music, with fans engaging in more concentrated listening and valuing the musical ideas and artistry involved. This highlights the genre's appreciation for complexity and artistic expression over popularity or background usage (Bačuvčík, 2010).

The "Bevorzugte Musikrichtungen nach Altersgruppen" study by the Deutsches Musikinformationszentrum is based on a representative sample of the German-speaking population aged 14 and over at their main residences in Germany. This comprehensive study reveals a decline in jazz popularity from 27.1 percent in 2003 to 25.2 percent in 2023. The highest levels of engagement are found among the 50–69 age groups, while the 14–19 age group exhibits the lowest at just 14.0 percent in 2023. Over the past 20 years, the 70+ age group has shown an 11.2 percent increase in jazz listeners, contrasting with significant declines among younger demographics, particularly those aged 20–39. These findings highlight the challenge jazz faces in attracting younger audiences despite its enduring appeal among older listeners in Germany (Deutsches Musikinformationszentrum, 2023). Given that Germany is one of the three largest recorded music markets in the EU, along with the UK and France (IFPI, 2024), we can reasonably assume that similar trends in jazz popularity and demographic engagement may be observed across the rest of the EU.

The IFPI "Engaging with Music 2023" statistical report reveals that Jazz is not among the top ten genres globally or in any other territory mentioned in the research, except for Indonesia, where it ranks as the ninth most popular genre (IFPI, 2023).

Despite the low ratings in the general research, jazz finds its place in a specific niche environment among collectors of physical records. The Discogs database, which serves as the marketplace for album collectors, lists 1,593,508 jazz releases, making it the fifth most represented genre, accounting for approximately 6.7 percent of all registered releases. For instance, rock holds the top spot with 6,455,271 releases (27.5 percent), followed by electronic with 5,152,106 releases (21.9 percent) and pop with 3,999,829 releases (17 percent) (Discogs, 2024).

The substantial number of jazz releases on Discogs.com underscores the genre's significant presence in music collections and the secondary market (Fig. 2.8). This suggests that while jazz may not be as commonly listened to as rock or pop in everyday contexts, it remains highly valued among collectors and enthusiasts, contributing to its prominent listing on Discogs[4] (Discogs, 2024).

The popularity of the physical format in the jazz genre is also visible in Nielsen Music's statistics, which list the format sales in various genres (Nielsen Music, 2018). Despite the digital age's proliferation, physical formats such as vinyl records and CDs continue to hold a special place in the hearts of jazz enthusiasts. Sales reports collected within the jazz genre reveal an interesting phenomenon—the enduring presence of physical products in the jazz recording market. According to Nielsen Soundscan from 2018, jazz as a genre still has a relatively high share of physical media sales in the U.S.A. compared to other sources of income in this

[4] The data were accessed on June 15th 2024 at Discogs.com.

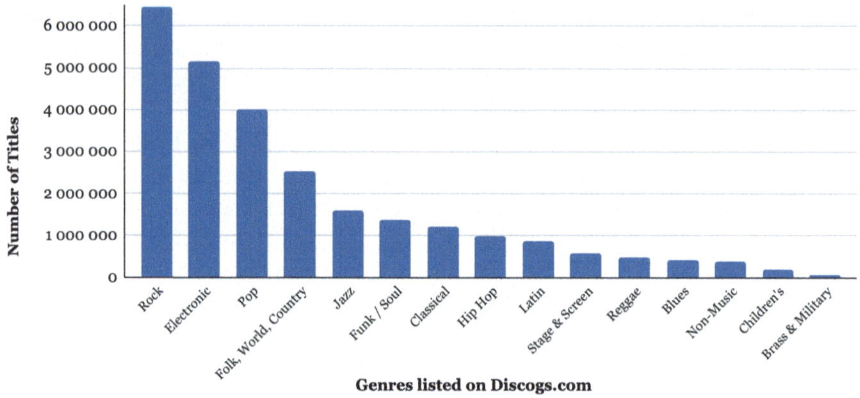

Fig. 2.8 Genres of titles listed in the Discogs database (Discogs, 2024)

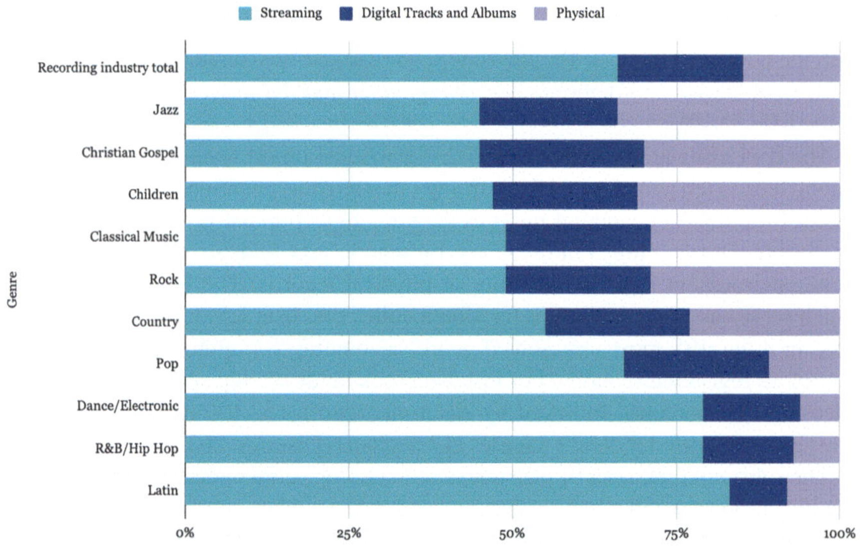

Fig. 2.9 Share of total audio album equivalent consumption by format in the U.S.A. in 2018 (Nielsen Music, 2018, processed by the author)

genre (digital downloads, streaming). In 2018, it was 34 percent in this given genre (jazz), in the case of R&B/Hip Hop, where it's only 8 percent of physical sales within this specific genre (Fig. 2.9).

However, according to 2020 statistics, the share of physical media sales in the U.S. jazz industry was much lower (Fig. 2.10). In 2020, in relation to other sources of profits, only 25.5 percent of physical media sales were earned. This means a decrease of 8.5 percent in 2 years. These changes are closely related to the ongoing digitization of music catalogs, easier access to music on streaming services, reduced costs for the production of music media, technological developments in music

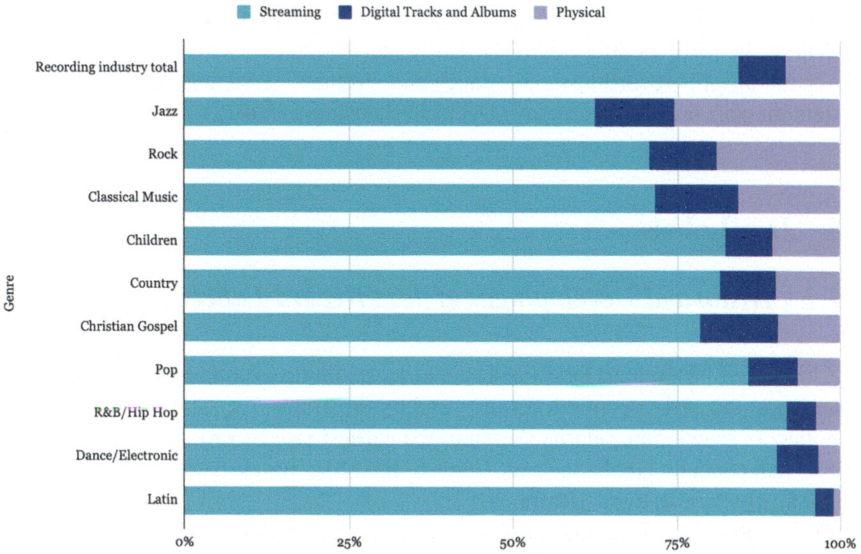

Fig. 2.10 Share of total audio album equivalent consumption by format in the U.S.A. in 2020 (MRC, 2021, 54)

playback devices, and the coming of a new generation of music users (MRC, 2021, 54).

Although statistics indicate that jazz is relatively low in global music consumption preferences (Fig. 2.7), the jazz community remains vibrant and active, organizing numerous conferences and events across the globe. In Europe, notable gatherings include *The European Jazz Conference* (Europe Jazz Network, 2024), *jazzahead!* in Germany (jazzahead!, 2024), *inJazz* in Rotterdam (inJazz, 2024), Netherlands, or the *Jazz Encounters* conference in Graz, Austria, focusing on research about jazz (Jazzforschung, 2024). Across the Atlantic, the United States hosts significant events, such as panel discussions during the *Winter Jazz Festival* (Winter Jazzfest, 2024). A key institution, *Jazz at Lincoln Center*, plays a crucial role in promoting and preserving jazz. Their mission is to entertain, enrich, and expand a global community for jazz through performance, education, and advocacy, with a belief that jazz serves as a powerful metaphor for democracy (Jazz at Lincoln Centre, 2024). As an example from the European context, Germany demonstrates its support for the jazz scene through various initiatives and awards, such as the *Albert-Mangelsdorff-Preis* and the *Deutsche Jazzpreis*. These efforts highlight the artistic achievements of jazz musicians and promote the genre both nationally and internationally. Despite these supportive measures, the "Jazzstudie 2022" by the *Deutsche Jazzunion*, a comprehensive survey, reveals significant economic challenges within the German jazz recording industry. Jazz musicians in Germany earn considerably less than the national average, a problem worsened by the COVID-19 pandemic, which led to fewer performance opportunities and recording sessions. Financial difficulties in the recording industry are further aggravated by limited funding and lower sales. Although there have been some improvements in gender diversity, structural inequalities still exist. The study calls for increased support, including better funding for recordings and venues and stronger social security measures to sustain the jazz scene in Germany (Deutsche Jazzunion, 2022).

2.7 Jazz Labels

2.7.1 Historical Development of Jazz Record Labels

The history of jazz record labels is fascinating, spanning over a century. Jazz music emerged in the early twentieth century, and by the 1920s, record companies began to notice its growing popularity. Some of the earliest jazz recordings were made by small, independent labels such as Gennett Records, Black Swan Records, ARC Records, or Okeh Records (Raffa, 2017).

One of the most important jazz record labels of the early years was Blue Note Records (now owned by UMG), which was founded in 1939 by Alfred Lion, Francis Wolff, and Max Margulis in the U.S.A. Blue Note became known for its high-quality recordings and its commitment to recording the best jazz musicians of the day. Some of the label's most famous artists included Thelonious Monk, Miles Davis, John Coltrane, and Art Blakey (ibid.).

In the 1940s and 1950s, other important U.S.-based jazz labels emerged: Prestige Records, Riverside Records, and Verve Records. These labels helped to document the emerging bebop and cool jazz styles of the time and featured artists such as Charlie Parker, Dizzy Gillespie, Miles Davis, and Bill Evans. Atlantic Records, another label in this period, signed Ray Charles, Charles Mingus, and various pop and R'n'B artists (Havers, 2023).

In the 1960s, jazz began branching into new styles, such as free jazz and fusion, and new labels emerged to support these new directions. Impulse! Records, founded in 1960–1961 by Creed Taylor (Waring, 2021), became known for its avant-garde jazz releases featuring artists such as John Coltrane and Pharoah Sanders. Other important labels of the era of the 1960s and 1970s included other labels in the U.S.A., for example, Nonesuch Records, Concord or Nine Winds, and labels based in Germany such as ECM Records, ACT Music, Winter & Winter or Enja Records (Hatteau, 2011).

In the 1980s and beyond, jazz continued to evolve and diversify, and new labels emerged to document these changes. In the U.S.A., Cadence Jazz and CIMP were founded in 1980 by Bob Rusch, growing out of the Cadence magazine and focusing on avant-garde jazz as well as Cuneiform, started by Steve Feigenbaum in 1984, focused on adventurous music blending jazz and rock (Hull, Unpublished). Besides the U.S.-based labels, there were many new companies emerging in the EU: Fresh Sound, founded in 1983 in Spain; Cris Cross in the Netherlands, founded in 1980; Nagel Heyer, founded in 1992 in Germany; and others (ibid.).

Today, there are countless jazz record labels around the world, both large and small, dedicated to promoting the diverse range of jazz music (Havers, 2023).

2.7.2 The Current State of Independent Jazz Labels

The state of independent jazz record labels in the recorded music industry is one of constant change and adaptation. While jazz music today has a dedicated and passionate fan base, it has usually not been as commercially successful as other genres, such as pop or hip-hop (MRC, 2021, 53).

As a result, jazz labels have had to be creative and flexible to survive and thrive in an ever-changing industry. One of the biggest challenges that jazz labels face today is the ongoing streaming trend. As more and more people turn to streaming services for their music consumption, jazz labels have had to adapt by making their music available and promoted on these platforms (McCain, 2023).

There are more issues that make today's independent jazz scene challenging. Jiwon Kwon's article "Where Is Jazz Going?: Reissues, Jazz Industry, and the Future of Jazz" discusses how the jazz industry's reliance on reissues of classic albums, such as those by John Coltrane and Miles Davis, impacts the growth of contemporary jazz artists. The article explores the historical roots of reissues, the role of educational institutions in jazz appreciation, and the industry's financial model, which favors reissues over new recordings, posing challenges for new artists. According to Kwon, the current state of the jazz industry reveals a paradox: the reverence for its rich heritage may impede its future growth. As Kwon (2020) articulates, the industry's financial dependence on reissues of classic albums by legends like John Coltrane and Miles Davis overshadows contemporary jazz innovations. This reissue-centric model, while profitable, marginalizes emerging artists who blend jazz with genres like electronic music and hip-hop. The historical roots of reissues and the role of educational institutions in promoting jazz appreciation have cemented a financial model that poses challenges for new artists to gain recognition and support (Kwon 2020).

The dominance of classic jazz icons on Spotify, like Ella Fitzgerald (4.83 million monthly listeners) and Stan Getz (4.45 million monthly listeners), underscores a critical challenge for contemporary jazz artists. According to Music Metrics Vault (Music Metrics Vault, 2024), historical figures still garner the most attention, making it difficult for modern innovators to gain the recognition they deserve. This streaming trend aligns with Jiwon Kwon's argument that the industry's focus on reissues hampers the promotion and growth of new jazz talent (Kwon, 2020). The same issue is mentioned in the study by George Tsang, "A Peep at the Current State of Jazz Music Through Data From Spotify (Part 1)" (2022). Moreover, this trend mirrors the broader shift towards catalog music consumption, which has increased significantly in recent years. In the U.S.A., "catalog music consumption increased from 61 percent in 2017 to almost 70 percent in 2021," meaning that only 30 percent of music consumption was of current releases. This trend poses a challenge to the sustainability and growth of contemporary jazz as newer artists struggle to gain the same level of exposure and support as established, often deceased, legends of the genre. These issues collectively underscore the difficulties faced by jazz music in maintaining its relevance and fostering new talent within the digital music landscape (Tsang, 2022).

Tsang highlights several challenges in the current digital landscape for jazz music. Firstly, "Spotify seems to associate jazz with artists who are not normally associated with jazz by any stretch of the imagination," leading to a misrepresentation of jazz in recommendations and playlists. This misclassification results in non-jazz tracks being more popular than actual jazz tracks, which is somewhat expected. Among the most popular tracks labeled as jazz, many are relatively new, with a significant number being Christmas songs that received a recent surge in plays. This raises concerns about the true representation of jazz music. Additionally, the categorization of artists like Norah Jones, whose music is "influenced by jazz" but not strictly jazz, complicates the genre's identity on streaming platforms (ibid.).

On the other hand, there are multiple organizations that are nurturing the contemporary jazz recording market. Besides the independent jazz labels that will be the subject of our study, we can name a number of other similar companies that exist in today's scene. Criss Cross Jazz, established in 1980 in Amsterdam, Netherlands; Cuneiform Records, founded in 1984 in Maryland, U.S.A., focuses on avant-garde and progressive music. Intakt Records, established in 1986 in Zurich, Switzerland; Mack Avenue Records, founded in 1999 in Michigan, U.S.A.; Ropedope, also established in 1999 in New Jersey, U.S.A.; MoonJune Records, founded in 2001 in New York, U.S.A.; Clean Feed Records, established in 2001 in Lisbon, Portugal; Motéma Music, founded in 2003 in San Francisco, U.S.A.; RareNoiseRecords, established in 2008 in London, UK; Edition Records, also founded in 2008 in Cardiff, UK; El Negocito Records, established in 2009 in Ghent, Belgium, and many other companies that bring new music rooted from the jazz tradition and beyond (Ricci & Racci, 2021).

Among the other notable independent jazz labels, 577 Records, Aguirre Records, Another Timbre, Ansible Editions, Arkeen, Astral Spirits, AUM Fidelity, Ayler Records, Biophilia Records, Bocian, Burning Ambulance Music, Carrier Records, Catalytic-Sound, Cellar Live, Chaikin Records, Chap Chap Records, Confront Recordings, Discreet Music, Discus Music, Enja & Yellowbird Records, Eremite Records, ESP-Disk, Firehouse 12 Records, Fundacja Słuchaj, Hat Hut Records, Hubro, Infrequent Seams, International Anthem, Jazz & People, Jazzland Recordings Norway, La Buissonne, Label Bleu, Libra Records, Luminous Label, Mahakala Music, Moserobie Music Production, Neither/Nor Records, NI VU NI CONNU, NoBusiness Records, Northern Spy Records, Not Two Records, Notice Recordings, OOYH Records, Origin Records, Pi Recordings, Posi-Tone, Pyroclastic Records, Qame Feraq, Raw Tonk Records, Relative Pitch Records, RogueArt, Royal Potato Family, Rune Grammofon, Screwgun Records, Silkheart Records, Skirl Records, Slow & Steady Records, Smoke Sessions Records, Stoned To Death, Sunnyside Records, Thanatosis, Thrill Jockey Records, Tripticks Tapes, Trost Records, Truth

Revolution Records, TUM, Tzadik, or Whirlwind Recordings stand out for their contributions to the jazz genre (Hillier, 2023).

Despite the challenges concerning the misclassification and the commercialization of the jazz genre, there are many reasons to be optimistic about the state of jazz record labels. Jazz music continues to attract new fans and create exciting new sounds, and many talented musicians and label executives are dedicated to keeping the genre alive, progressing, modifying, and, at the same time, preserving and celebrating this important musical tradition (Moore, 2021).

2.8 Strategies

As defined by the Cambridge Business English Dictionary, "Strategy" is "*the way in which a business, government, or other organization carefully plans its actions over a period of time to improve its position and achieve what it wants*" (Cambridge University Press & Assessment, 2024).

According to Lynch, every organization has three main areas of strategy to manage: its internal resources, the external environment within which it operates, and its ability to add value to what it does (Lynch, 2018).

As per BeStrategic Planning (2024), strategy operates at various organizational levels, each serving a unique purpose. These levels encompass the corporate, business, and functional tiers (bestrategicplanning.com 2024). However, it's essential to note that in our study, we will narrow our focus exclusively to the functional level. This focus is particularly relevant given that the companies under examination operate without the traditional corporate hierarchy, as they typically employ fewer than ten individuals. In such micro-businesses, the conventional distinction between corporate, business, and functional levels may not apply in the traditional sense. Therefore, our research will delve into the strategies adopted at the functional level within these smaller enterprises, providing insights into their decision-making processes and resource allocation methods, which are often more streamlined and adaptive due to their unique organizational context.

While this book is primarily centered on financial, distribution, product, and marketing strategies within the functional level of independent music labels, it's important to acknowledge the existence of other strategies that influence label operations. These may include human resource strategies, technology adoption strategies, and even legal and copyright strategies, among others. However, the reason for not making them the primary subject of this study lies in the recognition that financial, distribution, product, and marketing strategies are the cornerstones of a label's daily decision-making. These four areas have a direct and profound impact on a micro-label's ability to navigate a competitive music industry. Financial strategies determine resource allocation, distribution strategies define market reach, product strategies shape the label's artistic identity, and marketing strategies drive visibility. Given their fundamental role in the label's sustainability and growth, they warrant a comprehensive examination to uncover the distinctive approaches that empower independent music labels to excel within the constraints of their market. Nonetheless, the existence of other strategies remains a valuable aspect of the broader context in which these primary strategies operate.

While major corporations allocate substantial resources to the development of elaborate business strategies, this research focuses on a distinct category: independent jazz micro-labels. These agile entities operate within resource-constrained environments where adaptability and creativity are of paramount importance. In contrast to their larger counterparts, independent jazz record labels navigate the music industry with limited resources. Consequently, this study delves into the strategies that empower these labels to not only survive but thrive in today's dynamic and highly competitive music landscape.

The aim is to uncover the inventive tactics, adaptability, and innovative approaches that enable them to flourish and establish their presence in the world of music. Recognizing the unique challenges and opportunities that characterize the micro-business ecosystem, this study aims to shed light on the selected strategies by delving into their decision-making processes, resource allocation methods, and approaches to market positioning; this research seeks to uncover insights that can not only benefit individual micro-businesses but also contribute to the broader discourse on small business management and entrepreneurship.

2.8.1 Strategies in the Music Industry

The strategies of record labels, as elaborated in Peter Tschmuck's "Creativity and Innovation in the Music Industry" (2006), encompass various approaches across distribution, product innovation, marketing, and financial maneuvering to navigate the complex terrain of the music industry. Throughout the twentieth century, record label strategies evolved significantly in response to technological advancements and changing market dynamics. In the early twentieth century, the focus was primarily on sheet music and phonographs, with marketing efforts centered around live performances and radio. As the mid-twentieth century approached, the rise of radio and television became key promotional tools, marking the Rock 'n' Roll revolution and shifting the industry's focus to recorded music, establishing the phonographic industry at its core. By the late twentieth century, the emergence of the superstar model and market segmentation saw labels investing heavily in promoting a few successful acts to maximize returns. Entering the digital era, the rise of digital distribution and streaming services necessitated a significant shift in strategies as labels embraced new technologies and online marketing tactics to remain competitive in an increasingly digital landscape. This evolution reflects the industry's continuous adaptation to maintain market control while fostering innovation (Tschmuk, 2006).

Similarly, independent record labels in Poland face significant challenges due to declining physical record sales. The study "Running a Record Label When Records Don't Sell Anymore: Empirical Evidence from Poland" by Patryk Galuszka and Katarzyna M. Wyrzykowska (2016) highlights the innovative strategies these labels employ to survive. One prominent approach is the adoption of 360-degree deals, transforming labels into "music companies" that monetize various aspects of an artist's career, including recordings, live performances, and merchandising. This model, often initially applied to debut artists, allows labels to diversify their revenue streams (ibid.).

Additionally, some labels leverage artists' brand names to sell merchandise, a strategy particularly effective among hip-hop labels. Others target niche markets and formats, such as vinyl and cassettes, and sell music internationally, catering to a small but dedicated audience. A less structured "survival approach" involves conservative actions like renting recording studios and running music clubs. Despite these varied strategies, the core objective of promoting artists and their music remains intact, reflecting the industry's adaptability. The study underscores that while the traditional business model is evolving, the essence of managing a portfolio of artists persists, with future changes likely as streaming services become more prominent (ibid.).

2.8.1.1 Label's Goals

The music industry is a dynamic and ever-evolving landscape where success is often a subjective concept. According to Macy et al., determining what constitutes success in the music business is akin to chasing a moving target. This chapter delves into the diverse goals of independent record labels, exploring the spectrum of success that ranges from platinum-selling mainstream artists to grassroots, do-it-yourself musicians (Macy et al., 2016).

Defining Success

According to Rob Cannon's study "Beyond the Headlines: Media Representations of Artist Discourse on the Artist-Label Relationship" (2022), a successful record label is characterized by its ability to nurture and develop artist careers, providing essential support such as funding, marketing, promotion, and global distribution. Today's record labels play a crucial role in artist development, leveraging their expertise to market and promote music through both traditional and digital platforms. They handle the financial aspects of the music business, including providing advances and funding for recording sessions and managing the legalities of contracts and ownership rights. The primary goal of a record label, as outlined in Cannon's research, is to advance the careers of its artists while achieving commercial success, balancing creative needs with commercial objectives to foster long-term, successful partnerships. Ultimately, record labels aim to ensure that the music produced reaches the largest possible audience, generating revenue and enhancing their reputation in the industry (Cannon, 2022).

According to Macy et al., the answer to what defines general success in the music industry is often relative. On one hand, there are platinum-selling artists who have achieved household name status through mainstream recognition. On the other hand, we also find independent singer-songwriters who embody the do-it-yourself ethos. These artists traverse from venue to venue, performing numerous live shows and building a dedicated fan base through merchandise sales. The question arises: Is success somewhere in between, or does it depend on the unique goals and aspirations of each artist (ibid.)?

The stakeholders in this complex equation include both record labels and independent artists. For record labels, success may entail selling enough records to cover expenses, allowing the company to invest in emerging artists, pay employees, and sustain operations. On the other hand, for independent artists, success may be measured by the ability to create the music they desire, maintaining control over their artistic destiny, and making a living from their craft. According to Macy et al., the point of success lies in finding a balance where both record labels and artists are content with the outcome. If a record label can sustain its business model while supporting emerging talent, and if independent artists can maintain artistic control while making a living, it results in a win-win situation (Macy et al., 2016, 3).

2.8.1.2 Financial Strategy

The budgets of the recording production can vary significantly, ranging from under $50,000 to hundreds of thousands of dollars. Several factors contribute to this variation, with genres playing a crucial role. For instance, jazz recordings were typically done live with only a few takes, resulting in minimal studio and musician time. Country music, on the other hand, can range from simple to elaborate, sometimes approaching the higher budgets seen in pop or rock. Rap music can be relatively inexpensive, particularly when rappers already have their own rhythm tracks prepared in a project or MIDI studio. Conversely, it can become very expensive as numerous hours are spent creating beats, comping tracks, mixing, and remixing. For rock and pop genres, costs can also soar, especially when artists choose to write songs and work out arrangements in the studio or if the artist's musical and vocal abilities require additional time and resources (Hutchison et al., 2011, 217).

In light of digital technologies making the creation and distribution of masters easier and more cost-effective, the role of being a label, as described by Hutchinson, Strasser, and Hull, still revolves around obtaining masters through creation, purchase, or leasing. Subsequently, the label engages in distributing and marketing copies using various methods. However, due to the decline in high-revenue-producing CD sales, labels have taken measures to cut back on artist signings, big budgets, and substantial advances (ibid.).

According to Kwon (2022), the financial aspect of a jazz label's work has undergone a significant transformation, primarily influenced by the rise of digital streaming and the decline of physical album sales. Traditionally, jazz labels invested in the production of albums, covering costs such as studio time, musician fees, and manufacturing CDs or vinyl records. However, the shift to digital consumption has reduced these revenue streams, leading many labels to alter their financial strategies. For instance, labels like Sunnyside Records have moved towards licensing deals where the financial burden of recording is placed on the artists, who often seek external funding or self-finance their projects. In these arrangements, the label covers the costs of manufacturing, distribution, and marketing, taking on the risk that the album may not sell enough to recoup these expenses. Despite these challenges, the financial support labels provide—such as advances and handling of business logistics—remains a critical factor for many musicians, enabling them to focus on their creative pursuits while benefiting from the label's established distribution networks and promotional capabilities (Kwon, 2022).

Major Labels

The financial strategy of major record labels has undergone a significant transformation in response to the changing landscape of the music industry. Traditionally, label revenues heavily depended on CD and digital download sales. However, the rise of digital downloads, especially free downloading, led to a decline in album sales and an overall drop in music sales from its peak in 2000. In the face of this challenge, the 360-degree deal emerged as a strategic approach to adapt to the new reality. The 360-degree deal represents a shift in focus from solely relying on album and single sales to a more comprehensive revenue-sharing model. In a 360-degree deal, the artist shares profits from various income streams, including tour and merchandise revenue, corporate sponsorships, and publishing, in exchange for the upfront costs and marketing efforts provided by the record label. This approach enables labels to diversify their revenue sources and aligns the interests of the label with the overall success of the artist (Cole, 2010).

The music industry has witnessed a shift in artists' perceptions of record labels, with some exploring the DIY model. However, the challenges of managing various aspects of their careers, from A&R processes to marketing, make it difficult for artists to go completely independent. Deep pockets and expertise provided by labels remain crucial for artists aiming to achieve critical mass and become household names (Savage, 2022).

Macy et al. mention Pharrell Williams' success with the song "Happy" as an example of how artists can tap into multiple revenue streams. Beyond radio airplay, the song was featured in commercials, TV shows, and movies, generating income from various avenues. Pharrell's endorsement deals and ventures into fashion further showcase the potential for artists to maximize their financial gains beyond traditional music sales (Macy et al., 2016).

As the outlook for traditional record sales remains uncertain, the focus on sound recordings as a valuable asset for artists is more critical than ever. Record labels must navigate the evolving industry landscape, considering innovations and re-evaluating business models to ensure sustainable revenue streams. The role of publishing, as highlighted by the National Music Publishers Association (NMPA), underscores the importance of adapting to the new digital marketplace and addressing outdated copyright laws and regulations. The shift in royalty distribution over the past few years reflects the industry's response to changing dynamics. Mechanical sales (record sales) have lost ground, while performance royalties have increased significantly, indicating a need for performing rights organizations to adapt to emerging digital platforms and technologies (Macy et al., 2016).

Independent Labels

According to the World Independent Report Wintrends 2022, independent music companies are characterized by their diversified revenue streams, engaging in various business segments beyond sound recording. These include publishing, live events, merchandise, artist management, and distribution. Nevertheless, the core sound recording business, spanning digital formats, physical formats, and performance rights, remains the primary revenue driver for these companies. In 2020, the global sound recording business demonstrated a notable increase in sales. Notably, publishing, distribution, artist management, and merchandise segments displayed relative stability during this period, whereas the live and touring sector encountered significant challenges due to the profound impact of the COVID-19 pandemic (Worldwide Independent Network, 2022).

Digital formats emerged as the predominant revenue source for independent music companies within the sound recording domain, with consistent annual growth driven by the popularity of streaming. Both subscription-based and advertising-supported streaming categories continued to exhibit growth, solidifying digital as a cornerstone of financial success (ibid.).

The second most influential segment for sound recording revenues among independents was rights and licensing. Notably, the delay in the collection and distribution of performance rights revenues by collective management organizations mitigated the full impact of lockdowns and restrictions on companies in 2020. Interestingly, the physical market experienced marginal growth during the same period, driven by a resilient vinyl market, compensating for declining CD sales—a testament to the enduring strength of independent companies in this niche (ibid.).

In recent years, many independent jazz labels and artists in Europe have been seeking support for their projects through grants at different levels. These initiatives play a crucial role in providing financial assistance to sustain and promote the cultural richness of independent jazz projects in the region. One example can be programs of the German governmental organization Initiative Musik (Initiative Musik, 2024) or organizations such as Indieco, MES, Taike, and Suomenmusiikinkustantajat, which help indie labels in Finland by providing them with grant opportunities (Kumpunen, 2022, 50).

In his thesis "Sources of Income for Independent Record Labels," Nestori Kumpunen (2022) highlights the diversification of revenue through royalties, sync licensing, merchandise sales, physical sales, and live performances, although the COVID-19 pandemic necessitated new approaches such as streaming live events and seeking financial support through grants. Despite the significant impact of streaming, the sustainability of independent labels remains uncertain due to the competitive and rapidly evolving nature of the industry. Kumpunen concludes that while independent labels are essential for promoting artistic diversity and freedom, they face substantial challenges in achieving consistent financial stability, necessitating ongoing innovation and adaptation within the music business (Kumpunen, 2022).

2.8.1.3 Product Strategy

Hutchison et al. (2011) emphasize the product as an essential component of the marketing mix. They underscore the identification of underserved markets, characterized by unmet demands, as the cornerstone for the development of new products. Success in the marketplace, as outlined by the authors, hinges on a product's ability to align with its target market, exhibit uniqueness amidst competing offerings, and maintain an economically viable production process. The term "product" in the context of the music industry may evoke resistance among some artists who associate it with a departure from the essential nature of creative works. Nevertheless, as marketers frequently reference the sales volume of mass-produced copies, acknowledging the dual nature of music as both art and product becomes imperative for devising effective and sustainable product strategies in the dynamic music business landscape (Hutchison et al., 2011, 230).

In the music industry, the concept of a product extends beyond the produced music to encompass an artist's career and even an entire genre. This broader perspective includes an artist's image, persona, and narrative as integral components of the product offered to consumers. Notably, an artist's success can influence market dynamics for the entire genre, shaping audience preferences. For the purposes of this research, the primary focus will be on the product as an individual album release. By narrowing the scope to this specific aspect, the author aims to delve deeply into the strategies and considerations involved in the successful creation, promotion, and reception of album releases and their formats (ibid.).

In the modern recording industry, the Recording Industry Association of America (hereinafter referred to as RIAA) defines various digital and physical formats for music distribution, each emerging at different times. These formats include LP/EP and vinyl singles, which have been popular since the late 1940s. The eight-track format was prominent from the mid-1960s to the early 1980s, while cassettes and cassette singles were widely used from the 1960s through the early 2000s. CDs and CD singles have dominated from the 1980s to the present. SACDs and DVD audio were introduced in the late 1990s and early 2000s, respectively. Physical music videos have been available since the 1980s (RIAA, 2022).

With the advent of digital technology, newer formats include download albums and download singles, available since the early 2000s, and ringtones & ringbacks, which were popular in the 2000s. Download music videos and kiosks emerged in the 2000s. Paid subscriptions and on-demand streaming (ad-supported) became prominent in the 2010s, alongside other ad-supported streaming and SoundExchange distributions. Limited tier paid subscriptions were introduced in the 2010s, while synchronization has been in use since the mid-twentieth century (ibid.).

Physical Format

As highlighted in Sect. 2.2.1, "Current State of Recording Industry," 2023 marked the third consecutive year of growth for physical music formats (IFPI, 2024), with notable gains in CD revenue and continued expansion of interest in vinyl. This resurgence is not limited to just CDs and vinyl, as cassette tapes have also made a remarkable comeback, driven by nostalgia and a desire for tangible music experiences (Browne, 2022).

The vinyl revival has significantly impacted the industry, with demand now outpacing supply due to its appeal among both independent labels and major retailers. This trend has seen major labels and chain stores embrace vinyl as a growth sector, creating both market opportunities and production challenges. According to Palm (2017), Record Store Day has played a crucial role in boosting vinyl sales despite creating bottlenecks in the production process. This annual event, while elevating the profile and sales of vinyl records, has also driven up costs and strained the capacity of pressing plants, leading to delays and challenges for smaller independent labels trying to meet the surge in demand. The resulting pressure on the supply chain highlights the need for a sustainable production model that can support the resurgence of vinyl without compromising the industry's stability.

Despite the widespread adoption of digital formats, physical music offers distinct advantages that appeal to many consumers. Owning a physical album provides a tangible sense of permanence and personal investment that digital formats cannot replicate. Audiophiles often prefer vinyl records for their superior sound quality and the unique auditory characteristics, such as pops and hisses, that digital music lacks. Physical albums also include additional features like detailed artwork, liner notes, and bonus materials, enhancing the overall experience. The ritual of playing physical music evokes nostalgia and fosters a deeper connection to the music. While digital music is convenient, physical formats remain relevant for those who value these unique qualities. Ultimately, it is about aligning the product with the consumer's preferences, with no definitive right or wrong choice—only what best suits the individual (Daisie Team, 2023).

Digital Format

Digital formats encompass a variety of categories that have evolved over time. Download albums and singles have been available since the early 2000s, with ringtones and ringbacks gaining popularity during the same decade. Downloadable music videos and kiosks also emerged in the 2000s. The 2010s saw the rise of paid subscriptions and ad-supported on-demand streaming, along with other ad-supported streaming and SoundExchange distributions. Limited tier paid subscriptions were also introduced in the 2010s. Synchronization has been utilized since the mid- twentieth century. Guo (2023) highlights the growing popularity of various digital formats in music distribution—streaming services, digital downloads, social media platforms, or blockchain technology.

Streaming Services Platforms such as Spotify and Apple Music are highlighted for providing artists with substantial creative control and ownership of their copyrights. These services democratize access to music, allowing independent artists to reach broad audiences without traditional gatekeepers. However, they also reinforce the dominance of major corporations that aggregate and monetize niche audiences (Guo, 2023). Streaming has held an increasingly important position in the music market since 2004 and continues to drive the industry's revenue growth (Richter, 2024).

Digital Downloads Platforms like iTunes and Amazon Music facilitate direct purchases and downloads, offering artists a way to sell their music directly to fans. This format helps artists maintain more control over their revenue streams and provides consumers with permanent access to their purchased music files (Guo, 2023).

Social Media Platforms Due to their vast reach and direct audience engagement capabilities, social media platforms such as YouTube, Instagram, and TikTok have become crucial in music distribution and promotion. These platforms enable artists to create viral content and build fan bases organically. They are particularly popular for promoting new releases, live performances, and engaging with fans through comments and direct messages (ibid.).

Blockchain Technology Panzieri (2018) mentions the growing attention towards blockchain technology in music distribution and rights management. Blockchain platforms promise new models of artist compensation and distribution, potentially disrupting traditional music industry structures. By leveraging decentralized networks, these platforms aim to offer transparent and secure methods for distributing music and ensuring that artists receive fair compensation.

DIY and Independent Music Platforms The rise of platforms supporting DIY and independent music producers, such as Bandcamp and SoundCloud, is highlighted by Hesmondhalgh et al. (2019). These services empower artists to distribute their music without intermediaries, reflecting a growing trend toward self-publishing and direct fan engagement. These platforms allow artists to upload their music, set their own prices, and interact directly with their audience, fostering a closer artist-fan relationship (ibid.).

While these digital formats offer unprecedented opportunities, they also pose challenges related to sustainability and professionalization within the music industry (Panzieri, 2018). Furthermore, Panzieri suggests strategies for diversifying and supporting DIY and independent music scenes, such as community building, professional education, and creating access to professional services for those who cannot afford them.

Related Products

Merchandise has become a critical revenue stream for some independent record labels, especially as digital streaming dominates the music industry. By offering a range of products such as clothing (T-shirts, hoodies), accessories (hats, bags), and collectible items (posters, miniature figures), labels can generate significant additional income. Merchandise not only provides financial support but also strengthens the connection between artists and fans by offering tangible items that fans can use to express their support. Some labels manage their own merchandising efforts, while others partner with specialized merchandisers. The success of merchandise can be traced back to iconic examples like The Beatles in the 1960s, demonstrating its enduring potential. Creating and selling label-branded merchandise further helps raise awareness and establish a strong brand identity, making it a versatile and profitable venture for independent record labels (Kumpunen, 2022).

2.8.1.4 Distribution Strategy

Music distributors play a crucial role in facilitating the distribution of both physical and digital music to retailers. The rise of the Internet has led to the characterization of traditional stores as "bricks and mortar" establishments, drawing a comparison with the virtual retail market of online shopping. In the absence of distributors, the communication links between labels and retailers depend on the multiplication of the number of labels and the number of retailers. However, when a distributor is involved, this process is streamlined, resulting in a reduced number of contacts equal to the sum of labels and retailers (Hutchison et al., 2011).

David Hesmondhalgh et al. (2019) published a study about Bandcamp and SoundCloud as alternative music platforms from which independent labels can profit. To support and enhance revenue, an independent jazz label should leverage Bandcamp's strengths by utilizing it for direct sales of both digital and physical albums, as well as merchandise, creating unique storefronts for each artist, and offering exclusive content. They should adopt pricing strategies like the pay-what-you-want model and bundles to encourage larger purchases. On SoundCloud, the label should promote new releases by uploading tracks, live sessions, and curated mixes, fostering collaborations and remixes, and actively engaging with fans through comments and feedback (ibid.). Integrating social media for cross-promotion, hosting live streaming events and Q&A sessions, and developing a subscription model with exclusive content and community engagement will further deepen fan connections. Utilizing Bandcamp's analytics to optimize marketing strategies, building partnerships with other indie labels, and participating in jazz festivals will also expand their reach. These strategies collectively will help in effectively growing the label's revenue and building a loyal, engaged fan base (Hesmondhalgh et al., 2019).

In October 2023, Bandcamp laid off 50 percent of its workforce following its acquisition by Songtradr, a music licensing company. This decision was driven by the need to address Bandcamp's increasing operational costs and ensure financial sustainability. Despite significant reductions in staff across editorial, engineering, and support departments, Songtradr has committed to maintaining Bandcamp's core initiatives, including its artist-first revenue share model and Bandcamp Fridays.[5] The acquisition and subsequent layoffs have sparked considerable unrest among former employees and the broader music community (Ahmed & Tammet, 2023).

Physical Distribution

> "*It's been an honor to help so many artists like you sell CDs, vinyl, cassettes, and DVDs for the past 25+ years (...). As we turn this page in our history, we look forward to continuing to help you digitally distribute, market, and earn money from your music.*"—CD Baby in its letter to artists. (Purdy, 2023)

In the historical context of 2009, the retail landscape for physical records was characterized by a diverse array of store types, collectively representing 70 percent of album sales. This landscape included independent stores, "mom-and-pop" establishments, alternative outlets, and chain stores. Independent stores, tailored to specific music genres, accounted for 6 percent of sales, often distinguishing themselves through a focus on the used CD market (Hutchison et al., 2011).

The diagram below (Fig. 2.11) delineates the intricacies of music distribution across various channels, with a focus on the U.S.A.; however, a comparable system can be extrapolated for application in other territories. Noteworthy is the consolidation trend, which has significantly reduced the number of major labels possessing autonomous distribution capabilities, leaving three key players: Warner Music Group, Universal Music Group, and Sony Music Entertainment. These major labels also oversee "indie" distributors such as RED, Caroline, and ADA, which specialize in music from independent labels (Christman, 2011).

In "corporate distribution," the entire distribution channel, spanning from manufacturing to retail, is consolidated under a single business entity, exemplified by the Big Three label's nature. Contractual Distribution maintains individual operations within the distribution channel but establishes contractual relationships, fostering economies of scale for competitive pricing (Hutchison et al., 2011), as seen in retail co-ops. An example could be a big independent distributor, such as Believe, or one of the major label distributors for independents, such as ADA or The Orchard.

"Administered distribution" operates without formal contracts or corporate ownership, relying on the influence of a powerful member, such as major retailers like Walmart, to effectively control the distribution channel. Smaller businesses may engage with wholesalers or producers within administered systems, where influence often stems from sheer size (ibid.).

---

[5] "Launched in March 2020 during the Covid-19 pandemic, Bandcamp Fridays waive the platform's revenue share, directing all proceeds to artists and labels. This initiative has led to over $120 million being paid directly to musicians and record labels by millions of fans" (Bandcamp Staff, 2024).

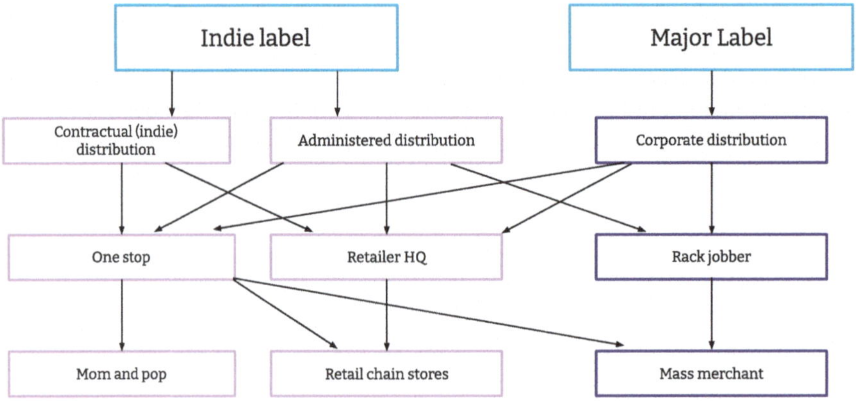

Fig. 2.11 Distribution channels for music products (Hutchison et al., 2011, 280, processed by the author)

Within this overarching framework, the distribution of the majority of recorded music unfolds through three primary channels: distributors, rack jobbers, and one-stops. A one-stop functions as a wholesale entity that curates products from diverse labels and distributors for resale to retailers, rack jobbers, mass merchants, and jukebox operators. While once primarily servicing jukebox operators, one-stops have evolved into crucial sources of products for small mom-and-pop retailers. Occasionally, major chains facing shortages of top-selling titles may turn to one-stops to bridge the gap until the arrival of their next shipment from the primary distributor (ibid.).

Concurrently, a rack jobber serves as a company that supplies records, cassettes, and CDs to department stores, discount chains, and other outlets. Specializing in providing the right music mix to enhance the music and/or video departments of these establishments, rack jobbers are particularly prominent suppliers for "big box" stores such as Walmart and Target (Hutchison et al., 2011).

The decline in CD sales at the beginning of the twenty-first century significantly impacted the traditional chain store model, leading to a reduction in the number of operating chains (Fig. 2.11). A notable example is Transworld Entertainment, the largest chain, which saw a substantial reduction from over 1000 stores in 2007 to 358 stores by 2013 (SeekingAlpha, 2013). This contraction reflected challenges in adapting to shifting consumer preferences and emerging alternative purchasing channels (Hutchison et al., 2011).

Concurrently, electronic superstores and mass merchants played an important role, strategically incorporating CDs into their offerings to contribute to 36 percent of album sales. Their retail strategies included employing alternative channels such as loss leader pricing for new titles and direct procurement from distributors. This era marked a transformative juncture in consumer behavior as alternative retail channels gained prominence, reshaping the dynamics of the music industry's retail landscape (Hutchison et al., 2011, 279–280).

A representative example is CD Baby, a pioneering web-based CD store launched in 1998, which initially focused on selling independent artists' physical CDs. However, by 2009, only 27 percent of its revenue came from physical sales. Simultaneously, CD Baby played a pivotal role in the digital music shift, becoming an early partner with the iTunes Store. During digital music's peak, it underwent acquisitions, first by Disc Makers and later by Downtown in 2019. With a lifetime payout of $600 million to artists, CD Baby decided in 2019 to close its online store, redirecting its focus to distribution, monetization, and promotion services. While still offering CD creation assistance, the company no longer facilitates CD sales, reflecting its adaptation to the evolving landscape of the music industry (Purdy, 2023).

However, as stated in Sect. 2.8.1.3.—Physical Format, "the physical music format has experienced a revival in recent years, marking its third consecutive year of growth in 2023" (IFPI, 2024). According to the School of Audio Engineering Institute (hereinafter referred to as SAE), vinyl records, or LPs, have experienced a notable resurgence over the past decade, characterized by a steady increase in sales that, in some instances, have even surpassed those of CDs. This revival is attributed to a blend of nostalgia, the appeal of a tangible music format, and the unique auditory experience that vinyl provides, which digital formats cannot fully replicate. High-profile releases from artists like Taylor Swift and Harry Styles have further propelled this trend, indicating vinyl's sustained relevance in the modern music industry (SAE Institute, 2023).

According to the Digital Entertainment and Retail Association (hereinafter referred to as ERA), CD sales in the UK have seen a resurgence, marking their first increase in two decades as of 2023. This renaissance is indicative of a broader trend in the physical music market, where overall spending on music formats such as streaming subscriptions, vinyl, CDs, downloads, and even cassettes grew by 9.6 percent in 2023. High-profile album releases and the enduring presence of physical retailers have significantly contributed to this renaissance, highlighting the continued relevance of CDs in the music industry (Paine, 2024).

Digital Distribution

Emerging technologies have opened new opportunities to DIY (do-it-yourself) and independent musicians, record labels, and formerly marginalized creators, offering them useful tools for both creation and audience engagement. Since the beginning of downloading and streaming culture, digital distribution has been the essential element for major and independent labels and artists to enter and operate in the recording industry (Mortimer et al., 2012).

Simultaneously, consumers now enjoy a large amount of diverse entertainment options. While these technological shifts have given rise to a modern golden age of creativity, the same advancements have also reshaped the competitive environment of the entertainment industry. Faced with these transformative changes, numerous organizations have encountered challenges that once compelled business leaders to navigate intricate tradeoffs between established models and emerging opportunities (Leea et al., 2016).

In April 2003, the introduction of Apple's iTunes Store marked the onset of the download era, establishing itself as the primary digital download platform. It distinguished itself by being the sole store to encompass the catalogs of all five major record labels, striving to offer a lawful alternative to illegal P2P (peer-to-peer) file-sharing platforms such as Napster or Pirate Bay. By 2008, iTunes had achieved the status of the leading music vendor in the United States, and by the early 2010s, it had secured its position as the largest global music vendor (Dechsakda, 2012, 3–6).

The ascent of Spotify in the realm of digital music distribution has been nothing short of remarkable. Founded in 2008 by Daniel Ek and Martin Lorentzon in response to the rampant piracy plaguing the music industry, Spotify initially offered a free service with ads, aiming to entice users into a subscription-based model. In the face of competitors like Apple Music and SoundCloud, Spotify has asserted its dominance by continually evolving its platform and adapting to industry shifts. However, not without controversy, the platform faced scrutiny from artists like Taylor Swift over compensation concerns, prompting Spotify to defend its model (BBC, 2018). Despite the ongoing tensions between Spotify's growth strategies and the financial well-being of artists and creators, the company remains an industry leader with 615 million monthly active users across 237 countries and territories. Spotify boasts a vast library of 100 million tracks and has a significant impact on the digital music landscape.

In the rapidly evolving landscape of digital music distribution, the predominant avenue for sharing music outside exclusive webshops or independent platforms is through Digital Service Providers (hereinafter referred to as DSPs). DSPs, such as Apple Music, Spotify, Deezer, and others, facilitate diverse digital music services, including streaming and downloads, across various devices (Songtrust, 2023).

The process typically involves uploading music to DSPs through distributors, entities that manage licensing, distribution to streaming services, and the payment of royalties to artists for streamed content. Beyond traditional major label structures, a multitude of distributors play pivotal roles in making music accessible to the public. Notable Artist Distributors (or so-called "Aggregators for Digital Music Distribution" like DistroKid, CD Baby, and EmuBands, are Record Union provide content upload and administration services (these distributors also often offer a label subscription model that is widely used by independent record labels). Label Distributors such as The Orchard, Believe, FUGA, and Symphonic contribute to widespread music distribution (these distributors usually collaborate on a contractual level). Additionally, Delivery Platforms like Audio Salad, Ampsuite, or Labelcamp assist artists who may not require assistance with the licensing side but need support in ensuring their music and metadata reach the intended destinations seamlessly (Spotify, 2024). These varied entities collectively contribute to the dynamic and expansive digital music ecosystem, offering artists a multitude of pathways to connect with their audiences.

Simultaneously, some of the DSPs offer access to streaming data and provide a variety of statistics and analytics to help musicians understand how their music is performing on the platform. These statistics are valuable for artists in making informed decisions about their marketing strategies, understanding their audience, and tailoring their music promotion efforts. Most DSPs also allow musicians and music creators to manage their presence on the streaming service and promote their other activities, such as live shows or the sales of merchandising. An example of the access hub is Spotify's Spotify for Artists or Apple Music's Apple Music for Artists (Warner, 2019).

The digital distribution of music provides countless opportunities for artists and labels to shape their approach to releasing and promoting their content. In the contemporary music industry, strategic playlist pitching can be considered a crucial element for artists and labels seeking to enhance their visibility and reach on streaming platforms. Playlisting, which involves curating and featuring songs in thematic or genre-specific playlists, provides a powerful avenue for music discovery. As streaming services like Spotify, Apple Music, and Tencent Music continue to dominate the digital music landscape, securing placement in popular playlists has become a significant factor in determining an artist's success. Playlist pitching, the process of submitting songs to be considered for inclusion in playlists, has evolved into a strategic promotional tool. Successful playlist placement not only exposes an artist's work to a broader audience but also contributes to increased streams and potential fan engagement. This shift in music consumption habits emphasizes the importance of understanding and leveraging playlisting dynamics as an integral component of contemporary music promotion strategies in the digital age. According to Chris Greenwood in Spotify Profits 2.0, the industry has moved to a "single economy"[6] (Greenwood, 2023).

Platforms like Apple Music and Amazon also offer features such as "instant gratification," enabling labels to pre-release selected singles from an upcoming album, creating anticipation, and using the single's distribution as a promotional tool. Some artists and labels also experiment with different timelines for physical and digital releases, exploring innovative strategies to maximize audience engagement and sales.

Delaying the Digital Release

A study discussed in the book "*Streaming, Sharing, Stealing*" highlights the importance of timely digital availability. The motion picture sales data from 2012 to 2013 reveal a significant downside to delaying digital availability, with almost a 50 percent reduction in digital sales when released after the DVD launch. Intriguingly, there was no statistically significant increase in DVD sales to offset this decline. The study underscores the risks associated with delaying digital availability,

[6] "Single economy" refers to the economic model in the streaming industry that is heavily reliant on the performance and revenue generated by individual tracks (singles). This model often emphasizes the success of hit singles over full albums, impacting how artists release music and earn revenue.

emphasizing that without a robust digital platform, major players in the industry may miss out on crucial benefits tied to digital distribution (Smith & Telang, 2017).

The study identifies five key benefits of digital distribution, emphasizing its pivotal role in the industry. These include the ability to evaluate the potential market for content more effectively, efficiently promote content to consumers, conduct and learn from detailed experiments on consumer responses, retain data on individual customers, and observe data related to customers' behavior towards the product. Understanding and leveraging these benefits is crucial for labels seeking to navigate the dynamic landscape of digital music distribution successfully. The fundamental insight for the entertainment industry is that future success hinges on companies not only maintaining control over content production but also establishing control over the interface with their customers. This includes overseeing the data derived from understanding their customers' needs. The ability to directly manage the customer interface and leverage customer data is increasingly vital for navigating the evolving landscape of the entertainment business (ibid.).

The Waterfall Release Strategy on Spotify

> "*Albums don't sell albums; singles sell albums.*"—Chris Greenwood.

According to Chris Greenwood, the Waterfall Release Strategy is the best way to release songs on Spotify. This method involves releasing multiple singles leading up to a full-length album or EP release. The key element of this strategy is consistency, which includes releasing a new song every 6–8 weeks, each supported by a strong marketing campaign. Greenwood also highlights the use of tools such as playlist editorial pitching and Release Radar, which require submitting music well in advance and emphasizes the importance of planning and patience (ibid.).

2.8.1.5 Marketing Strategy

Marketing strategy is a set of decisions and actions taken by a company's marketing department to promote the company's products or services to potential customers and achieve its marketing objectives. A marketing strategy is developed based on the company's overall business strategy, target market, marketing channels, marketing mix, and competitive environment (Macy et al., 2016, 115).

Record labels have evolved their marketing strategies from focusing on the phonograph as a luxury item to leveraging broadcasting and, later, music videos and social media to promote music. The symbiotic relationship between small independent labels and radio stations in the late 1940s and onwards highlighted the importance of airplay for record sales. Marketing strategies further transformed with the advent of music television channels like MTV, emphasizing the critical role of visual media in music promotion. These strategies underscore the industry's adaptability to new promotional platforms and the importance of radio and video in the marketing mix (Tschmuck, 2006).

This research will focus mostly on marketing not as a comprehensive management concept but as a sales policy instrument used to increase record sales. The chapters dedicated to marketing strategy will be closely related to the previously mentioned product strategy, as product analysis is the key activity in creating a marketing plan (Macy et al., 2016). The marketing plan, according to Macy et al., should provide all basic information about the release. This means everything related to the product identity (album and artist's name, bios), timeline and pricing (street date, discounts), stock information (barcodes, quantities, format), marketing goals and objectives (target market), promotion and publicity (information about singles, schedules, promotional activities, target media outlets, ad schedule), advertising (materials, content), sales (sales forecast, account-specific promotions), video, tour support among others. Macy et al. point out the importance of timing the street date, considering holiday seasons and strategic release of the singles weeks (Macy et al., 2016).

All this data, representing the product, is subsequently used for planning a strategic marketing campaign. The following paragraphs will focus on establishing the terminology for digital marketing. Given the modest contribution of physical sales to the overall industry revenue (IFPI, 2024), the subsequent chapter will exclude discussions on physical marketing.

Digital Marketing

The thesis by Eemeli Bodde provides specific examples of digital marketing strategies utilized by music industry professionals through social media platforms. For instance, it mentions the strategic use of Facebook for organizing and promoting events, engaging with fans through direct communication, and building online communities. Instagram is highlighted for its ability to visually showcase artists' work, behind-the-scenes content, and live performances, fostering a parasocial interaction between artists and fans. TikTok is noted for its unique approach to content creation, where users engage with music through short videos, dance challenges, and lip-syncs, offering a platform for songs to go viral and reach a global audience rapidly (Bodde, 2023).

An online blog Gitnux offers a comprehensive strategy for record label marketing that thrives on digital engagement and sophisticated audience targeting. The core of the strategy leverages social media for direct engagement, employs targeted advertising to reach potential fans with precision, and embraces influencer collaborations to boost artist visibility. Email marketing and strategic public relations complement these efforts, establishing a direct line to fans and enhancing the label's profile through media coverage. Additionally, partnerships and content marketing deepen the narrative around artists, while live events and grassroots promotions engage local fan bases (Key Record Label Marketing Strategies [Recent Analysis], 2023).

Streaming platforms, Search Engine Optimization (hereinafter referred to as SEO), and music licensing emerge as critical tools for enhancing online visibility and diversifying revenue streams. Optimizing playlists and metadata on streaming services ensures artists are easily discoverable, while SEO tactics aim to boost the label's search engine rankings. Licensing deals extend the reach of music into new markets and mediums, bolstering exposure and opening up new financial avenues (ibid.).

At its heart, the strategy focuses on building a vibrant community around the label's brand, fostering a sense of loyalty and belonging among fans through exclusive content, meetups, and incentives. This approach, as outlined by Gitnux, blends traditional marketing methods with digital innovations, navigating the complexities of the modern music industry to effectively promote artists and engage audiences (ibid.).

The Playlist Pitching and Third-Party Playlist Promotion

Playlist pitching refers to the process of submitting music to the curators of in-house (editorial) playlists managed by streaming services. This practice is a continuation of traditional music promotion strategies, where rights holders advocate for the inclusion of their music based on its quality and predicted value, similar to how they would seek to get music on radio playlists or in the press (Morgen, 2022, 151–169).

In a handbook "*Work Hard Playlist Hard*," Warner (2019) categorizes playlists on streaming services into four main types: Editorial, User (Third Party), Brand, and Tastemaker. Editorial playlists are curated by the platform's internal team, providing significant exposure for featured artists. User (Third Party) playlists are created by individual users or independent curators, offering a diverse range of music. Brand playlists are managed by companies or influencers, often reaching large audiences through their established followings. Tastemaker playlists are curated by influential individuals within the music industry, whose selections can significantly impact an artist's career. Each type offers unique opportunities and requires different strategies for artists aiming to be featured (Warner, 2019, 9).

The study by Benjamin A. Morgen (2022) highlights that pitching to in-house (editorial) playlist curators is typically done by established industry professionals, such as record labels, managers, and digital aggregators, who have the necessary connections and relationships with the curators. This process is distinguished from third-party playlist promotion, where external user-generated playlists are targeted for music placement, often involving financial transactions to secure a spot on these lists (ibid.). The optimal timeframe for submitting a music release is typically advised to be at least 1 month in advance, primarily due to the intricacies of the pitching process. Editors responsible for curating tracks for editorial playlists appreciate having ample time to thoroughly assess the submitted music, considering the volume of submissions they need to review. Providing accurate and comprehensive information to these editors is crucial, and transparency in responses is highly valued. Enhancing the submission process involves highlighting key marketing features of the project, allowing it to stand out amidst other song suggestions. Greenwood further suggests establishing a more personalized connection with head editors, fostering a deeper understanding of the artist's profile, and establishing a lasting rapport for future pitching endeavors (Greenwood, 2023).

Artist Profiles on Social Media and DSPs

Numerous blogs and articles offer insights into effective self-promotion strategies on streaming services. Warner (2019), emphasizes the significance of establishing a robust online presence. This involves not only maintaining profiles on social media platforms such as Facebook, Twitter, LinkedIn, Instagram, and TikTok, but also optimizing profiles on streaming services. Platforms such as Spotify for Artists or Apple Music for Artists provide artists with editable profiles, allowing them to actively engage with their audience, enhance visibility, and cultivate a dedicated fan base (Warner, 2019).

According to Greenwood in Spotify Profits 2.0 (2023), it is essential to maintain the artist profiles on Spotify and use their potential via artist banners, image galleries, merch sales, or concert announcements so the artists can get more involved with their fans. Another useful tool is "The Artist Pick"—a feature that allows the artist to control the music that appears at the top of their artist profile and even showcase their merchandise there. The Artist Pick only lasts 14 days, so it requires an active approach to keep this feature used (Greenwood, 2023).

Spotify also enabled a feature called "Canvas," which is a 3- to 8-second visual loop the artist/label can create that plays while the song is being played, filling a vertical mobile phone screen. Statistics mentioned in the article of Digital Music News mentioned that Canvas increased shares by 145 percent and playlist adds by 20 percent (Murphy, 2022).

Greenwood emphasizes the crucial role of maintaining a connection with fans through social media and underscores the significance of consistency in the long-term process of building a community (Greenwood, 2023).

Spotify Ads

According to Chris Greenwood in his handbook "*Spotify Profits 2.0: Music Marketing and Business Strategies for the New Singles Economy*," (2023), Spotify ads are a recommended tool for musicians and labels aiming to grow their audience, increase streaming numbers, promote merchandise, and boost tour attendance. Greenwood points out that when ads are placed on platforms like Facebook or Instagram, there is the challenge of convincing potential fans to switch platforms, which introduces friction and reduces the campaign's effectiveness. Spotify ads, however, eliminate this barrier by reaching users who are already in a music-listening mindset, thereby increasing the chances of interaction with the artist's music (Greenwood, 2023, 49).

Greenwood recommends a multifaceted strategy for using Spotify ads, which centers around building a long-term fan base rather than seeking immediate returns.

He notes that while an immediate return on investment may not be visible within the first few months, the ads are crucial for creating momentum. A core aspect of Greenwood's strategy is the precise targeting and tailored content of the ads. He advises that when creating a Spotify ad, it is essential to identify and target fans of similar artists. This increases the likelihood that the music will resonate with the listeners. Additionally, he emphasizes the importance of crafting a compelling call to action within the ad script. This directive encourages listeners to engage further by clicking through to the artist's profile, album, or playlist, thereby driving up streaming numbers (ibid., 50).

Greenwood also finds Spotify ads effective for promoting merchandise and tours. He recommends targeting ads at "warm and hot" audiences—those already familiar with the artist—to drive sales of merchandise by offering special deals or exclusive items. Similarly, he suggests using geo-targeted ads to promote upcoming tours and shows, ensuring that only fans in relevant areas see the promotions, which increases ticket sales and event attendance, offering incentives like VIP experiences or exclusive merchandise. Furthermore, Greenwood emphasizes the importance of continuous testing and adjustment. He advises monitoring ad performance metrics like click-through rate and making necessary adjustments to ensure that the campaigns are effective (ibid., 58).

Another significant element of Greenwood's strategy is leveraging Spotify's algorithm. He highlights that a key goal is to achieve a popularity score that triggers Spotify's algorithm to include the artist's music in coveted algorithmic playlists like Discover Weekly or Release Radar. This organic inclusion can exponentially increase streams and expose the music to a broader audience without additional advertising costs (ibid., 56).

In summary, Greenwood presents Spotify ads as a powerful marketing tool due to their ability to target engaged listeners within the platform, the long-term strategy of building a dedicated fan base, and the meticulous approach to ad creation and performance monitoring. By investing in Spotify ads, Greenwood suggests that musicians and labels can ensure their music reaches the right audience, steadily grow their listener base, effectively promote merchandise and tours, and ultimately sustain their careers in the competitive music industry (ibid.).

Sources

Ahmed, A., & Tammet, D. (2023). Bandcamp lays off half its staff after buyout by Songtradr. The Guardian. https://www.theguardian.com/music/2023/oct/17/bandcamp-lays-off-half-its-staff-after-buyout-by-songtradr

Anderton, C., Dubber, A., & James, M. (2013). *Understanding the music industries*. SAGE.

Arditi, D. (2021). *ITake-Over: The recording industry in the streaming era*. Lexington Books.

Bačuvčík, R. (2010). *Jak posloucháme hudbu? Vztah obyvatel České republiky k hudbě a jejímu poslechu 2009*. VeRBuM.

Bandcamp Staff. (2024). *This Friday is Bandcamp Friday*. Bandcamp Daily. https://daily.bandcamp.com/features/bandcamp-fridays-in-2024

Bartmanski, D., & Woodward, I. (2020). *Labels: Making independent music*. Bloomsbury Academic.
BBC. (2018). *How Spotify came to be worth billions*. BBC. https://www.bbc.com/news/newsbeat-43240886
Bell, T. L., & Johansson, O. (Eds.). (2016). *Sound, society and the geography of popular music*. Taylor & Francis Group.
Bodde, E. (2023). *Utilizing social media platforms in Music marketing*. Tampere University of Applied Sciences.
Browne, D. (2022). Cassette tapes are making a comeback. Rolling Stone. https://www.rollingstone.com/music/music-features/cassette-tape-comeback-walkman-1234606978/
Cambridge University Press & Assessment. (2024). STRATEGY | English meaning – Cambridge dictionary. Cambridge Dictionary. https://dictionary.cambridge.org/dictionary/english/strategy
Cannon, R. (2022). Beyond the headlines: Media representations of artist discourse on the artist-label relationship. **IASPM Journal*, 12*(1), 3–26. https://doi.org/10.5429/2079-3871(2022)v12i1.2en
Carter, E. (2024). Poverty among riches: Understanding the contracted economy for recorded music and its impact on market actors. *Journal of Cultural Economy, 17*(3), 345–359. https://www.tandfonline.com/doi/abs/10.1080/17530350.2024.2302152
Catalano, T. J. (2023). Microenterprise: Definition, types, example – business. Investopedia. https://www.investopedia.com/terms/m/microenterprise.asp
Christman, E. (2011). What exactly is an independent label? Differing definitions, different market shares. Billboard https://www.billboard.com/music/music-news/what-exactly-is-an-independent-label-differing-definitions-1177068/
Cole, T. (2010). You ask, we answer: What exactly is a 360 Deal? NPR. https://www.npr.org/sections/therecord/2010/11/24/131574836/you-ask-we-answer-what-exactly-is-a-360-deal?t=1650279435162
Crane, D. (1976). Reward systems in art, science and religion. *The Production of Culture, 19*(6), 57–62.
Daisie Team. (2023). Pros & cons of physical vs digital Music distribution. Daisie Blog. https://blog.daisie.com/pros-cons-of-physical-vs-digital-music-distribution/#pros-of-physical-music-distribution
Dechsakda, R. A. (2012). *The effects of digital Music distribution*. Southern Illinois University Carbondale.
Deutsche Jazzunion. (2022). Jazzstudie 2022. Deutsche Jazzunion. https://www.deutsche--jazzunion.de/jazzstudie-2022/
Deutsches Musikinformationszentrum. (2023). Bevorzugte Musikrichtungen nach Altersgruppen. https://miz.org/de/statistiken/bevorzugte- musikrichtungen-nach-altersgruppen.
Dias, J., & Medbøe, H. (2014). Improvisation in the digital age: New narratives in jazz promotion and dissemination. *First Monday, 19*(10). https://doi.org/10.5210/fm.v19i10.5553
Discogs. (2024). *Exploring Jazz on Discogs*. https://www.discogs.com/search/?ev=em_rs&genre_exact=Jazz
Europe Jazz Network. (2024). European jazz conference 2024: Tomorrow comes today | Europe jazz network. Europe Jazz Network |. https://www.europejazz.net/press-release/european-jazz-conference-2024-tomorrow-comes-today
European Commission. (2020). *User guide to the SME definition*. Publications Office of the European Union.
Galuszka, P., & Wyrzykowska K. M. (2016). Running a record label when records don't sell anymore: Empirical evidence from Poland. *Popular Music, 35*(1), 23–40. https://doi.org/10.1017/S0261143015000811
Gioia, T. (2017). *How to listen to jazz*. Basic Books.
Greenwood, C. (2023). *Spotify profits 2.0: Music marketing and business strategies for the new singles economy*. Chris Greenwood.
Guo, X. (2023). The evolution of the Music industry in the digital age: From records to streaming. *Journal of Sociology and Ethnology, 5*(10), 7–12. https://doi.org/10.23977/jsoce.2023.051002

Hatteau, B. (2011). Jazz news: ENJA records' Matthias Winckelmann interviewed at all about jazz! All About Jazz. https://www.allaboutjazz.com/news/enja-records-matthias-winckelmann-interviewed-at-all-about-jazz/
Havers, R. (2023). The history of recorded Jazz | uDiscover. uDiscover Music. https://www.udiscovermusic.com/in-depth-features/the-history-of-recorded-jazz/
Hayes, J. (2020). State of the industry: Major label vs. non-major label regional performance. Hypebot. https://www.hypebot.com/hypebot/2020/01/state-of-the-industry-major-label-vs-non-major-label-regional-performance.html
Hesmondhalgh, D. (2021). Is music streaming bad for musicians? Problems of evidence and argument. *New Media & Society, 23*(12), 3593–3615.
Hesmondhalgh, D., Jones, E., & Rauh, A. (2019). SoundCloud and Bandcamp as alternative Music platforms. *Platformization of Cultural Production, 1*(13), 1–13. https://doi.org/10.1177/2056305119883429
Hillier, N. 2023. Discover the best independent jazz labels | Bestofjazz.org. Best of Jazz. https://bestofjazz.org/the-best-independent-jazz-labels/#full
Hitters, E., & den Drijver, R. (2017). The business of DIY. Characteristics, motives and ideologies of micro-independent record labels. *Cadernos de Arte e Antropologia, 6*(1), 17–35. https://doi.org/10.4000/cadernosaa.1192
Hutchison, T. W., Strasser, R., & Hull, G. P. (2011). *The Music business and recording industry: Delivering Music in the 21st century*. Routledge.
IFPI. (2023). Engaging with Music 2023. IFPI. https://www.ifpi.org/wp-content/uploads/2023/12/IFPI-Engaging-With-Music-2023_full-report.pdf
IFPI. (2024). Global Music Report 2024. IFPI. https://ifpi-website-cms.s3.eu-west-2.amazonaws.com/IFPI_GMR_2024_State_of_the_Industry_db92a1c9c1.pdf
Initiative Musik. (2024). *Initiative Musik*. Initiative Musik: Startseite. https://www.initiative-musik.de/
inJazz. (2024). About. injazz. https://www.injazz.nl/about/
Jazz | English meaning – Cambridge Dictionary. (2023). Cambridge Dictionary. https://dictionary.cambridge.org/dictionary/english/jazz
Jazz at Lincoln Centre. (2024). Mission & Values. Jazz at Lincoln Center. https://jazz.org/about-us/mission-values/
Jazzahead. (2024). About Us jazzahead! — jazzahead! https://jazzahead.de/about-us/
Jazzforschung. (2024). Jazz Encounters. Institut 16 Jazzforschung. https://jazzforschung.kug.ac.at/events/vera
Kees, I. N. (1998). The compact disc story. *JAES, 46*(5), 458–460, 462, 464, 465.
KEF. (2024). Hidden Mavericks of Music: Notable Indie record labels you need to know. Sound of Life. https://www.soundoflife.com/blogs/mixtape/indie-record-labels
Key Record Label Marketing Strategies [Recent Analysis]. (2023). The Gitnux Blog. https://blog.gitnux.com/strategies/record-label-marketing-strategies/
Kordestani, M. (2022). What is the role of a record label in Today's Music business? Rolling Stone. https://www.rollingstone.com/culture-council/articles/what-is-the-role-of-record-label-in-todays-music-business-1234588863/
Kumpunen, N. (2022). *Sources of income for independent record labels*. Tampere University of Applied Sciences. https://www.theseus.fi/bitstream/handle/10024/752634/Kumpunen_Nestori.pdf?sequence=3&isAllowed=y
Kwon, J. (2020). Where is jazz going?: Reissues, jazz industry, and the future of jazz | FUSION. FUSION Magazine. https://www.fusionmagazine.org/where-is-jazz-going-reissues-jazz-industry-and-the-future-of-jazz/
Kwon, J. (2022). Freedom and control: Musicians' A ol: Musicians' autonomy and record labels' influence in producing the sound of contemporary jazz. In *Washington university open scholarship*. Washington University in St. Louis. https://openscholarship.wustl.edu/cgi/viewcontent.cgi?article=3783&context=art_sci_etds

Leea, M., Choia, H. B., Choa, D., & Lee, H. (2016). Cannibalizing or complementing? The impact of online streaming services on Music record sales. *Elsevier B.V. T, 91*, 662–671.

Lynch, R. (2018). *Strategic management*. Pearson Education Limited.

Macy, A., Rolston, C. P., Allen, P., & Hutchison, T. W. (2016). *Record label marketing: How Music companies brand and market artists in the digital era*. Focal Press.

McCain, A. (2023). 30+ Harmonious Music industry statistics [2023]: Worth, data, and revenue. Zippia. https://www.zippia.com/advice/music-industry-statistics/

Meeder, C. (2012). *Jazz: The basics*. Taylor & Francis.

Meltzer, D., ed. (1993). *Reading Jazz*. San Francisco: Mercury House.

Micro Business Development Program | Department for Children and Families. (2023). Vermont Department for Children and Families (DCF). https://dcf.vermont.gov/benefits/MBDP

MIDiA Research. (2024). Music streaming services subscribers market shares 2023. Music Industry Blog. https://www.statista.com/statistics/653926/music-streaming-service-subscriber-share/

Monson, I., Early, G., & American Academy of Arts & Sciences. (2019). Why Jazz still matters. *Dædalus S, 148*(2), 7. 10.1162.

Moore, M. J. (2021). In 2021, jazz went back in time to see the future. NPR. https://www.npr.org/2021/12/20/1064066269/in-2021-jazz-went-back-in-time-to-see-the-future

Morgen, B. A. (2022). Optimisation of musical distribution in streaming services: Third-Party playlist promotion and algorithmic logics of distribution. In G. Morrow, D. Nordgård, & P. Tschmuck (Eds.), *Rethinking the Music business: Music contexts, rights, data, and COVID-19*. Springer International Publishing. https://doi.org/10.1007/978-3-031-09532-0_9

Mortimer, J. H., Nosko, C., & Sorensen, A. (2012). Supply responses to digital distribution: Recorded music and live performances. *Information Economics and Policy, 24*(1), 3–14. ISSN 0167-6245.

MRC. (2021). 2020 MRC data year-end charts. *MCR data year-end report U.S. 2020 presented in collaboration with Billboard*, 53.

Murphy, C. J. (2022). Spotify canvas: Increase your track shares by 145%. Digital Music News. https://www.digitalmusicnews.com/2022/03/07/spotify-canvas/

Music & Copyright. (2021). UMG and SME put the market share squeeze on WMG and the independent sector. Music & Copyright's Blog. https://musicandcopyright.wordpress.com/2021/04/21/umg-and-sme-put-the-market-share-squeeze-on-wmg-and-the-independent-sector/

Music & Copyright. (2023). Market share—Music & Copyright's blog. Music & Copyright's Blog. https://musicandcopyrightwordpress.com/tag/market-share/

Music Metrics Vault. (2024). *Most popular jazz artists on Spotify*. Music Metrics Vault. https://www.musicmetricsvault.com/genres/jazz/339

Nielsen Music. (2018). Mid-year report U.S. 2018. Nielsen. https://www.nielsen.com/wp-content/uploads/sites/2/2019/04/us-midyear-music-report-2018.pdf

Nwagwu, W. E., & Akintoye, A. (2023). Influence of social media on the uptake of emerging musicians and entertainment events. *Information Development, 40*(4), 667–692. https://journals.sagepub.com/doi/pdf/10.1177/02666669221151162

Office Of Advocacy. (2023). Small business facts: The role of microbusiness employers in the economy. U.S. Small Business Administration. https://advocacy.sba.gov/2017/08/01/the-role-of-microbusiness-employers-in-the-economy/

Paine, A. (2022). Music week. Music Week. https://www.musicweek.com/labels/read/independent-labels-market-share-set-to-increase-for-fifth-consecutive-year/086968

Paine, A. (2024). ERA: CD sales increase for the first time in 20 years. Music Week. https://www.musicweek.com/labels/read/era-cd-sales-increase-for-the-first-time-in-20-years/089068

Palm, M. (2017). Analog backlog: Pressing records during the vinyl revival. *Journal of Popular Music Studies, 29*, e12247. https://doi.org/10.1111/jpms.12247

Panzieri, G. (2018). DIGITIZATION, SUSTAINIBILITY AND PROFESSIONALIZATION IN THE MUSIC INDUSTRY new strategies for diversification and support for DIY and independent Music scenes. Academia. https://www.academia.edu/39195899/DIGITIZATION_SUSTAINIBILITY_AND_PROFESSIONALIZATION_IN_THE_MUSIC_

INDUSTRY_New_strategies_for_diversification_and_support_for_DIY_and_independent_music_scenes

Paul, A. S. (2019). Aggregation services and songwriter independence. *Capstone Projects and Master's Theses*. 680. https://digitalcommons.csumb.edu/caps_thes_all/680?utm_source=digitalcommons.csumb.edu_percent2Fcaps_thes_allpercent2F680&utm_medium=PDF&utm_campaign=PDFCoverPages.

Pokorná, A. (2024). *Value gap v hudebním streamingu*. Online. Bachelor these. Brno: Janáčkova akademie múzických umění, Hudební fakulta. Available at: https://is.jamu.cz/th/nw0b3/.

Priest, E. (2021). The future of music Copyright collectives in the digital streaming age. *The Columbia Journal of Law & Arts, 45*(1).

Purdy, K. (2023). End of an era: CD baby stops distributing artists' CDs, vinyl, and other goods. Ars Technica. https://arstechnica.com/culture/2023/05/end-of-an-era-cd-baby-stops-distributing-artists-cds-vinyl-and-other-goods/

Raffa, M. (2017). Jazz and the disc: Media, labels, producers. A century-long relationship. In *In a century of jazz. Impromptu creativity*. Skira. https://www.researchgate.net/profile/Massimiliano-Raffa/publication/361248599_Jazz_and_the_disc_media_labels_producers_A_century-long_relationship/links/62a5f1676886635d5cd41eb5/Jazz-and-the-disc-media-labels-producers-A-century-long-relationship.pdf

Resnikoff, P. (2018). Collectively, indie labels are now bigger than any major label. Digital Music News. https://www.digitalmusicnews.com/2018/05/20/indie-labels-major-label/

RIAA. (2022). U.S. Music Revenue Database. RIAA. https://www.riaa.com/u-s-sales-database/

Ricci, M., & Racci, V. (2021). Best jazz record labels article. All About Jazz. https://www.allaboutjazz.com/top-jazz-record-labels-2020

Richter, F. (2024). Infographic: Streaming drives global Music industry to new highs. Statista. https://www.statista.com/chart/4713/global-recorded-music-industry-revenues/

Rodičová, J. (2015). Comparison of Music preferences of university students in The Czech Republic and other European Union countries. *Music Preferences of Youth as a Contemporary Music Education Issue, 264*(26), 67–77. https://doi.org/10.5817/CZ.MUNI.P210-8108-2015

SAE Institute. (2023). Return of vinyl and physical Music | insights | SAE blog. SAE Institute. https://www.sae.edu/gbr/insights/the-return-of-vinyl-analysing-the-resurgence-of-physical-music-formats/

Savage, M. (2022). More and more musicians are releasing their own music: Here's why. BBC. https://www.bbc.com/news/entertainment-arts-60051802

Schafer, B. (2021). Where will Spotify be in 5 years? The Motley Fool. https://www.fool.com/investing/2021/04/15/where-will-spotify-be-in-5-years/

SeekingAlpha. (2013). *Trans world entertainment: Transformation in decline*. Nasdaq. https://www.nasdaq.com/articles/trans-world-entertainment-transformation-decline-2013-03-19.

Semancik, A. (2024). How AI is transforming the creative economy and music industry. Ohio University. https://www.ohio.edu/news/2024/04/how-ai-transforming-creative-economy-and-music-industry

Smith, M. D., & Telang, R. (2017). *Streaming, sharing, stealing: Big data and the future of entertainment*. MIT Press.

Songtrust. (2023). MUSIC PUBLISHING GLOSSARY – Digital Service Provider (DSP). Songtrust. https://www.songtrust.com/music-publishing-glossary/glossary-digital-service-provider

Soundcharts Team. (2022). A complete guide to Music distribution companies. Soundcharts. https://soundcharts.com/blog/music-distribution

Spotify. (2024). Kyle McEvoy. Spotify. https://open.spotify.com/artist/6rRqxCKHpl9C5Imf2uinft

Statista. (2024). *Global record companies market share 2023*. Statista. https://www.statista.com/statistics/422926/record-companies-market-share-worldwide-physical-digital-revenues

Stone, J. (2020). *The state of the Music industry in 2020*. Toptal. https://www.toptal.com/finance/market-research-analysts/state-of-music-industry

Taylor, T. D. (2015). *Music and capitalism: A history of the present*. University of Chicago Press.

The Intellectual Property Office. (2019). *Music 2025: The Music data dilemma: Issues facing the music industry in improving data management*. The Intellectual Property Office.

Tsang, G. (2022). A peep at the current state of jazz music through data from Spotify (part 1). George Tsang. https://tsanggeorge.medium.com/a-peep-at-the-current-state-of-jazz-music-through-data-from-spotify-part-1-75400069f2dc

Tschmuck, P. (2006). *Creativity and innovation in the Music industry*. Springer.

Tschmuck, P. (2021). *The economics of Music*. Agenda Publishing.

Walzer, D. A. (2017). Independent music production: How individuality, technology, and creative entrepreneurship influence contemporary music industry practices. *Creative Industries Journal, 10*(1), 21–39.

Waring, C. (2021). *Impulse for change: A short history of impulse! Records*. uDiscover Music. https://www.udiscovermusic.com/in-depth-features/story-of-impulse-records/

Warner, M. (2019). *Work hard playlist hard: The DIY playlist guide for artists and curators*. Tablo Publishing.

Wikström, P. (2014). *Ch@nge: The Music industry in an age of digital distribution*. BBVA Open Mind. https://www.bbvaopenmind.com/wp-content/uploads/2014/04/BBVA-OpenMind-The-Music-Industry-in-an-Age-of-Digital-Distribution-Patrik-Wikstrom.pdf

Winter Jazzfest. (2024). Jazz Talks 2024 — Winter Jazzfest. Winter Jazzfest. https://www.winterjazzfest.com/jazz-talks-2024

Witt, S. (2015). *How Music got free: What happens when an entire generation commits the same crime?* Penguin Random House.

Worldwide Independent Network. (2022). Wintrends 2022. Winformusic.org. https://winformusic.org/mp-files/wintrends-2022.pdf/

Chapter 3
Findings

Abstract The chapter "Findings" is structured into two main sections, each offering detailed insights into different aspects of the music market and the strategies employed by independent jazz micro-labels. The first section, "Trends and Suggested Strategies," examines the trends appearing in the current independent music industry. This part of the chapter is informed by the author's interviews with professionals specializing in independent digital distribution and by the author's desk research.

The second section, "Strategies of Independent Jazz Micro-Labels," focuses on the specific approaches adopted by representatives of independent jazz micro-labels. It explores the challenges and opportunities faced by these micro-labels and how they leverage their specialized knowledge and resources. By examining these strategies, the chapter aims to provide substantial information that addresses the research questions, offering insights into the operational tactics and strategic decisions of independent jazz micro-labels in the contemporary music market.

3.1 Trends and Suggested Strategies in the Digital Landscape

This chapter delves into the prevailing trends and strategic recommendations within the music industry based on comprehensive research and interviews with industry professionals. We explore how independent record labels navigate the evolving landscape of physical and digital formats, focusing on effective strategies to maximize revenue and market reach.

M. Drnek Bóková, *Strategies of Micro-Enterprises in the Recording Industry*, Music Business Research, https://doi.org/10.1007/978-3-031-88439-9_3

3.1.1 *Financial Strategies: Sources of Income in the Digital Music Sector*

The insights from the interview with Kervin M. Dockendorf shed light on diverse sources of income in the digital music sector. Licensing emerges as a crucial revenue stream, encompassing agreements for short films, feature films, and video games (interview with the author, June 26, 2023).

The interviewee underscores the significance of a popular social media platform, TikTok. While TikTok itself might not directly generate revenue, its ability to propel a song to viral fame creates a pathway for users to migrate to other platforms such as Spotify, Apple Music, or Amazon, leading to potential song purchases (ibid.).

The interview also highlights Facebook's role in the digital music landscape, specifically through Prime Music videos, emphasizing that their monetization is currently limited to the United States and Mexico (interview with the author, June 26, 2023). Furthermore, Dockendorf emphasizes the enduring importance of concerts, particularly for jazz musicians, and the synergy between licensing, streaming, and live performances, reinforcing the idea that the digital music landscape thrives on a multifaceted approach to income generation (ibid.).

Kyle McEvoy provides a detailed perspective on the diverse sources of income available in the digital music sector, emphasizing both traditional and modern avenues. One of the key insights he shares is the shift from waiting for large, sporadic sync deals to capitalizing on numerous smaller opportunities. McEvoy explains that some companies now maintain extensive music libraries used by hundreds of thousands of subscribers for platforms like YouTube, which allows artists to earn steady, albeit smaller, income streams. This method contrasts sharply with the traditional approach, where artists wait for a significant sync opportunity in TV or film, which might take a year or more (ibid.). McEvoy touches upon the importance of microsync deals for smaller artists. He notes that while the revenue from these deals isn't massive, they provide consistent income and ensure that the artist's music is being actively used across various social media platforms and other digital content, which can accumulate to a significant amount over time (ibid.).

Streaming revenue is another critical income source highlighted by McEvoy. He discusses how collaborations and remixes can extend the reach and longevity of a piece of music, thus enhancing streaming numbers and revenue. By having other artists remix tracks and releasing these as new collaborations, McEvoy's label has successfully broadened the audience and cross-pollinated fan bases, leading to increased streaming and revenue potential (ibid.).

McEvoy additionally underscores the flexibility and artist-friendly nature of his label's deals, where artists retain their publishing rights and own their masters. This approach, which he contrasts with traditional 50/50 deals that can significantly cut into the artist's earnings, is seen as a more sustainable and appealing model for artists in the digital age. These artist-friendly deals also include the fact that the label doesn't invest in the music's production and instead serves as a mediator between the artist and the distribution company, thereby allowing artists greater creative control and a larger share of the financial returns from their work (ibid.).

In summary, McEvoy's insights highlight income opportunities through digital platforms, focusing on remixes and collaborations for wider audience engagement, micro-sync licensing for consistent, small-scale revenue from content usage, and direct artist-platform relations for greater control and efficiency. These strategies underscore the shift towards digital-centric models, leveraging technology and digital content strategies to maximize revenue and artist empowerment (interview with the author, March 28, 2024).

The Orchard's Naemi Wetter emphasizes the importance of digital streaming platforms (DSPs) such as Spotify, Apple Music, and Deezer as primary revenue sources for labels and musicians, highlighting their dominance due to large user bases and regional preferences. While mechanical and performance rights contribute to income, DSPs generate the most significant revenue (interview with the author, July 16, 2024).

Wetter points out that the performance of DSPs varies significantly by territory. For instance, Spotify is the dominant platform in Germany, while Deezer still holds substantial influence in France, and Apple Music has a stronger presence in the U.S.A. than in Germany. This regional variation necessitates a tailored approach to digital music distribution, ensuring that strategies are adapted to the preferences and behaviors of users in different markets. Wetter notes the varying payout structures across different distribution services and the advantage of having personalized support from larger distribution companies, which can offer better deals and more tailored metadata management compared to DIY platforms like DistroKid (ibid.).

Wetter places significant importance on social media platforms, specifically TikTok and Instagram, as crucial tools for reaching new audiences and boosting engagement (ibid.).

3.1.2 Digital Distributors' Challenges in Collaboration with Record Labels

Dockendorf points out common mistakes made by record labels in collaboration with digital distributors. One prevalent issue is the last-minute delivery of masters, with labels sometimes expecting a quick release, even with minimal notice. Dockendorf highlights the challenges of such situations, recognizing that labels often face their own time constraints driven by deadlines or partnerships.

Another significant oversight he observes is the lack of a coherent strategy. Some labels seem to believe that merely releasing music, regardless of its quality, will naturally lead to success. Dockendorf mentions the importance of strategic thinking, urging labels to invest more time in planning and considering potential actions, target audiences, and overall strategy. He encapsulates this sentiment with the adage, "*If you fail to plan, you plan to fail,*" emphasizing the critical role of thoughtful planning in achieving successful music releases.

Dockendorf highlights additional challenges in the collaboration between digital distributors and record labels. One recurring issue is receiving incorrect masters, where labels sometimes realize they've sent the wrong files on the day of release, necessitating urgent audio replacements. In more extreme cases, Dockendorf has encountered instances where labels unintentionally send him music from one artist but later discovered it belongs to someone else entirely. This mishap results in a race against time to rectify the error before the song's scheduled release (interview with the author, June 26, 2023).

On a more positive note, Dockendorf acknowledges instances where success seemed serendipitous, occurring without extensive planning. He recounts a scenario where a meeting 2 days before a song's release led to subsequent support for every subsequent release. However, he also emphasizes the significance of disciplined labels and artists who meticulously plan and follow timelines, acknowledging that, despite these efforts, success isn't guaranteed. In the unpredictable music industry, he notes that even with careful planning and diligent efforts, a song's success ultimately depends on its resonance with the audience, underlining the subjective and unpredictable nature of musical success in the market (ibid.).

Kyle McEvoy addresses several significant external challenges that digital distributors face when collaborating with record labels. One of the primary issues he highlights is the tension between maintaining the independent ethos of digital distribution and the commercial pressures exerted by major labels (interview with the author, March 28, 2024).

Furthermore, McEvoy discusses the competitive landscape where major labels, recognizing the shrinking gap in market share between independent and major label releases, are increasingly buying up independent distributors. This trend, according to McEvoy, is an attempt by major labels to regain control and market share, which paradoxically undermines the very independence that these distributors are supposed to support (ibid.).

Another critical challenge involves the operational complexities and financial pressures that arise as labels grow. McEvoy points out that larger labels often struggle with the logistical aspects of managing royalties and accounting, which can become a "mess" as more money starts moving around. This issue is compounded by the need to keep artists happy, which McEvoy suggests is best achieved through artist-friendly deals that offer flexible distribution rates and allow artists to retain their rights (ibid.).

McEvoy also notes the importance of direct relationships between artists and platforms, predicting that the future will see more direct distribution models that bypass traditional middlemen entirely. He envisions a scenario where technology enables artists to distribute their music directly to all platforms, thereby simplifying the process and reducing the need for intermediary distribution companies (ibid.).

Naemi Wetter highlights several challenges digital distributors face when collaborating with record labels. One of the main issues is labels "not being ahead" of their metadata, often resulting in errors like incorrect ISRC codes being assigned to releases. Additionally, the lack of sufficient lead time for new releases is a significant problem, as distributors need ample time to prepare and promote new music effectively. Wetter also notes that labels sometimes provide inaccurate information and fail to act on suggestions provided by distributors, leading to missed opportunities for optimization and promotion (interview with the author, July 16, 2024). This complements Dockendorf's observations about receiving incorrect masters, which can necessitate urgent audio replacements on the day of release (interview with the author, June 26, 2023).

Another major challenge is the varying levels of engagement and motivation among labels. Some labels do not follow through with the recommendations and strategies provided by the distributor, which hampers the overall success of campaigns. Wetter emphasizes that the distributor's level of engagement often mirrors that of the label; the more motivated and active the label, the more the distributor can support them effectively (ibid.).

In conclusion, the collaboration between record labels and digital distributors is challenging due to issues like last-minute delivery of masters, incorrect file submissions, and a lack of strategic planning. Success in the music industry often hinges on careful planning and adherence to timelines, though it remains unpredictable. External pressures, such as major labels acquiring independent distributors, complicate the landscape and undermine the independence valued by artists. Effective collaboration requires accurate metadata, sufficient lead times, and active engagement from labels to optimize promotional efforts and ensure successful music releases (ibid.).

3.1.3 Independent Digital Distribution Options and Their Dis/Advantages

In the interview with Kervin M. Dockendorf discussing digital distribution options, he emphasizes the accessibility of digital aggregators such as DistroKid, CD Baby, Amuse and similar services. For a modest fee, anyone can release their music independently. However, Dockendorf points out that this approach might be limited, as these services generally don't offer additional support, such as playlist pitching or further guidance (interview with the author, June 26, 2023).

On the other end of the spectrum, larger distributors like Red Eye Worldwide (independent) or The Orchard (owned by a major label) may not be feasible for everyone. They often require a minimum monthly income to consider a label or an artist, as they invest time and resources in those they represent. Dockendorf acknowledges the necessity for such companies to ensure a viable business model (ibid.).

In contrast to both distributing options mentioned above, Dockendorf's company occupies a middle ground. Reflecting on his role, Dockendorf acknowledges that his company may not have the influence of larger distributors, but it offers a more personalized approach compared to widely accessible services. He describes his company as not being as big as industry giants but as providing a level of personalized service beyond the reach of more mainstream options. One key advantage he highlighted is the direct communication and personalized support he offers to artists and labels. This stands in stark contrast to larger platforms where artists might feel like just another number. This accessibility, where artists can chat, call, or message you for instant assistance, is a significant benefit mentioned by those who transition from automatized services like DistroKid (ibid.).

Naemi Wetter highlights several key advantages of working with The Orchard as a distributor. She notes that The Orchard, being tied to Sony Music Entertainment, secures better deals with individual digital service providers (DSPs) compared to smaller independent distributors, resulting in higher payout rates for artists and labels. Wetter emphasizes the personalized support offered by The Orchard, which includes real people who can handle specific metadata requirements and provide tailored adjustments for releases, unlike the automated systems of DIY platforms like DistroKid (interview with the author, July 16, 2024).

Wetter also points out the benefits of collaboration and data insights at The Orchard. The distributor actively encourages artist collaborations, amplifying their reach and engagement. Additionally, The Orchard's vast amount of data and expertise from different territories provides valuable insights and specific advice for promotional activities, radio pitching, and live gigs (ibid.).

She further notes that The Orchard offers a robust infrastructure, including services that are often unavailable or require additional payment on DIY platforms. This includes better workstations and tools for collaborators, enhancing overall efficiency and effectiveness. Moreover, Wetter highlights the flexibility The Orchard provides in managing audio and metadata. For instance, artists can easily replace audio files without the need for a complete takedown and re-upload, which is a cumbersome process on platforms like DistroKid (ibid.).

3.1.4 Marketing Within Streaming Platforms and Social Media

In the conversation with Kervin M. Dockendorf about marketing on streaming platforms such as Spotify, Apple, Tidal, etc., he highlighted some interesting points. He acknowledged that running ads on TikTok can be costly, but he emphasized its potential to make a song go viral, which can be a game-changer for attracting listeners. However, he also questioned whether this strategy is feasible for smaller niche labels due to the limited audience size (interview with the author, June 26, 2023).

Shifting focus to Spotify, Dockendorf shared insights beyond the elemental playlist pitching. He mentioned opportunities where you can purchase or reserve specific spaces, like a header for a particular territory. The "catch" is that you need to apply for these opportunities at least 6 weeks in advance. Similar promotional tactics exist on iTunes and Apple Music, involving banners on the home screen or within specific music genres. Dockendorf noted that these strategies are widely adopted by most distributors and have proven to be effective in boosting visibility and driving sales (ibid.).

Dockendorf's insights into communication with Digital Service Providers (DSPs) for marketing placements within streaming platforms illuminated the competitive nature of securing those coveted spots. He acknowledges the challenges artists face in this pursuit, noting that DSPs may reject a song for various reasons, such as not fitting their preferences or not gaining traction within a week (ibid.).

Dockendorf underscores the importance of driving external traffic to the platform, increasing the likelihood of editors or algorithms taking notice. To achieve this, he sometimes employs Facebook and Instagram ads with a smart link, directing traffic to the artist's profile or a curated playlist. While the immediate income from streaming may be modest, Dockendorf emphasizes the long-term benefits, describing it as a "long tail income" or "long-term royalties." He highlights that, despite a slower start, the continuous and lasting nature of streaming income can contribute to sustained revenue over time (ibid.).

Dockendorf advocates allocating a substantial portion of used finances, approximately 25 percent of the project budget, to digital marketing. He strongly advises against engaging with external services that promise placement in numerous playlists, cautioning that many of these services employ bots and can jeopardize an artist's standing on platforms like Spotify due to artificial numbers. Dockendorf recounts instances where artists attempted to inflate their perceived popularity through such services, only to face repercussions, including potential bans from the platform (ibid.).

He underscores the producer's ability to initiate collaboration with an artist whose work has the potential to gain an audience, emphasizing that quality content will eventually find its audience without resorting to artificial tactics. Dockendorf encourages a pragmatic approach, suggesting the release of compilations and/or compiling tracks that didn't make it into individual albums, creating a cohesive and value-added product (ibid.).

Kyle McEvoy offers a nuanced view of marketing within streaming platforms, emphasizing the importance of distinctive artist attributes and robust data to stand out in a crowded field. McEvoy points out that streaming platforms like Spotify and Apple Music receive thousands of pitches daily from various artists and label representatives. To effectively market within these platforms, he underscores the necessity of providing compelling statistics and unique artist features that differentiate them from others. This involves highlighting achievements such as significant social media engagement, viral content, or high numbers of song saves, which can capture the attention of platform editors (interview with the author, March 28, 2024).

Additionally, McEvoy, similarly to Dockendorf, stresses the importance of organic growth overpaid social media marketing. He advocates for artists to focus on maintaining a strong and consistent presence on platforms like TikTok and Instagram, which involves regular posting and engagement rather than relying on paid advertisements. This approach, he believes, is more effective in building a genuine connection with the audience and fostering long-term growth (ibid.).

As mentioned in the previous chapter, McEvoy also highlights the power of collaborations and remixes in expanding an artist's reach. By working together with other artists, particularly in creating new versions of existing songs, artists can tap into each other's fan bases, thereby broadening their audience and increasing their visibility on streaming platforms. This strategy not only boosts streaming numbers but also enhances the overall marketability of the music (ibid.).

Wetter underscores the necessity of maintaining up-to-date and well-managed artist profiles across all platforms to maximize opportunities. Naemi Wetter points out that many artists and labels tend to focus heavily on Spotify while neglecting their profiles on other streaming platforms like Deezer and Tidal. She emphasizes the importance of maintaining up-to-date and well-managed profiles across all platforms, not just Spotify. This includes regularly updating artist pictures, ensuring correct releases are mapped to the pages, and utilizing features like artist-curated playlists. Neglecting these other platforms can result in chaotic profiles, which may lead to missed opportunities for support and visibility, especially in more niche genres where platforms other than Spotify can play a crucial role. Wetter stresses that keeping profiles clean and up-to-date across all streaming services is essential for maximizing reach and engagement. Artists should curate their DSP biographies, naming similar artists or influences to help in searches and improve visibility in the "Fans Also Like" section. "*Just use everything they (DSPs) offer because the algorithm will see it, and it will reward you,*" states Naemi Wetter (interview with the author, July 16, 2024).

Wetter also speaks about the importance of adapting to new Spotify features to maximize visibility and engagement. She highlights tools like Canvas and music videos, which can enhance algorithmic support for tracks. Maintaining a well-curated Spotify biography and using promotional tools like Spotify Marquee and Showcase are crucial for reaching and expanding an artist's audience. Additionally, she advises incorporating comprehensive campaign strategies that go beyond Spotify ads (such as connecting the ad to an anniversary edition of a physical format or similar), utilizing all available features such as live dates and Shopify integration to fully leverage the platform's potential. She highlights the importance of using a direct link to the purchase page, emphasizing the need to eliminate any additional "clicks" to streamline the purchasing process (ibid.).

Furthermore, Naemi Wetter mentions the significant role that artist collaborations play in maximizing visibility and engagement in the digital music sector. She suggests that musicians should actively support each other through initiatives such as account takeovers, where one artist logs into another's social media profile for a day to post content. This strategy helps introduce fans to new artists and creates a sense of community and shared audience (ibid.).

Additionally, Wetter recommends that artists curate their own playlists, combining their music with tracks they personally enjoy or believe their fans would appreciate. This not only enhances the listening experience but also helps the algorithm recognize connections between different songs and artists, potentially boosting streaming numbers (ibid.).

Wetter also mentions the role of Facebook groups, WhatsApp communities, and Discord channels for niche genres and fan engagement. These platforms allow artists to maintain close contact with their fans, fostering a sense of community and special treatment. Artists can post daily updates, interact directly with superfans, and create a more personal connection (ibid.).

These collaborative efforts are particularly beneficial for independent and niche genre artists who may not have the extensive marketing resources of larger labels.

By leveraging each other's audiences and creating authentic, engaging content, artists can enhance their reach and build a stronger, more interconnected fan base. This strategy aligns with Wetter's broader advice on the importance of maintaining an active and well-curated presence across all digital platforms to maximize revenue and engagement opportunities (ibid.).

In summary, the interviews with the digital distributors provide a comprehensive overview of effective marketing strategies for music on platforms like Spotify, Apple Music, and Tidal. They emphasize the potential of TikTok ads to make songs go viral, though their high cost may be prohibitive for smaller labels. Purchasing promotional spaces like headers on Spotify requires advanced planning, and it is similarly effective on iTunes and Apple Music. Maintaining updated and well-managed artist profiles across all streaming platforms is crucial for maximizing visibility and engagement. Organic growth through collaborations, remixes, and artist-curated playlists is emphasized over artificial playlist placement services. Driving external traffic to streaming platforms via social media ads and smart links is vital for long-term streaming income. Building strong fan communities on platforms like Facebook, WhatsApp, and Discord enhances engagement and support. Leveraging new features like Spotify's Canvas, Marquee, and Showcase, along with comprehensive campaign strategies, can boost an artist's reach. The chapter underscores the importance of a multifaceted and genuine approach to marketing within streaming platforms, focusing on long-term benefits and authentic audience connections.

3.2 Strategies of Independent Jazz Micro-Labels

With the rise of digital music platforms and social media, independent jazz micro-labels find new avenues to connect with audiences and build their brand. However, the independent label landscape is complex and constantly evolving, and success requires a careful balance of entrepreneurialism, creativity, and business acumen. In this chapter, we explore the strategies used by independent jazz micro-labels to thrive in the modern music industry, from creating strong products to navigating digital distribution and marketing. The following insights are informed by semi-structured interviews conducted with nine representatives from independent jazz micro-labels based in the EU and the U.S.A. By understanding these strategies, we gain insight into the unique challenges and opportunities facing independent jazz micro-labels.

This chapter is divided into five subchapters, each delving into a critical aspect of independent jazz record micro-labels. The first subchapter focuses on the label's goals and visions, providing context and understanding of their foundational motivations and the nature of their operations. This foundational knowledge is essential for appreciating the unique character and ambitions that drive these labels.

The second part examines the importance of the physical and digital products. This includes a detailed look at the label's relationships with streaming services and their evolution since these platforms emerged. Additionally, this section investigates the extended assortment that micro-labels in jazz offer to their customers, showcasing how they diversify their offerings to cater to niche markets.

The third subchapter is dedicated to distribution strategies. It explores the relationships independent labels maintain with their distributors and how their approaches shift over time. This analysis sheds light on the logistical challenges and innovative solutions these labels employ to get their music to the audience.

The fourth subchapter focuses on the labels' financial aspects. Here, we answer questions about the labels' income channels and the nature of their deals with artists. This section provides a comprehensive overview of the financial mechanisms that sustain independent labels and ensure their profitability and sustainability.

The final subchapter focuses on marketing strategies, particularly within streaming platforms and social media. It also discusses traditional PR services and events as tools to market the label's music. This section aims to reveal how independent labels leverage both modern and traditional marketing techniques to enhance their visibility and reach in a crowded market.

3.2.1 Goals and Visions

The author considers the goals of independent record labels essential when discussing their strategies. Knowing organizations' goals can help us understand why they make certain decisions and how they approach their business operations. The goals of independent jazz record labels can vary widely depending on factors such as the label's purpose, size, history, funding, genre focus, and target audience. Here are some examples of the different goals that independent jazz record labels may have. In most cases, the goals of the interviewed labels are combined:

Discover and Promote New Talent Some independent jazz record labels are mainly focused on finding and promoting emerging jazz musicians who have not yet had a chance to record or release their music. They may see their role as discovering and nurturing new talent in the jazz world. All labels interviewed for this book share this goal.

Provide a Platform for/from a Developed Musician Some independent labels are built around an advanced career of one musician or one band who prioritizes artistic and entrepreneurial freedom to an extensive network of a major label. This kind of enterprise is represented in this study by Heartcore Records, founded by guitarist Kurt Rosenwinkel, Razdaz Recordz, founded by bass player Avishai Cohen, and Greenleaf Music, founded by trumpet player Dave Douglas. All these labels are also focused on finding and developing new talents and presenting fellow artists to their fan base.

Similar examples from the past could be Charles Mingus' and Max Roach's Debut Records, Horace Silver's Silveto, or Gene Russel's Black Jazz Records. At present, there are many jazz independent labels of this kind, such as Tim Berne's Screwgun, John Zorn's Tzadik, drummer John Bishop's Origin Records, and Hopalit Records by German pianist Pablo Held.

Filling a Gap in the Scene of a Specific Territory, Subculture, or Genre Some independent jazz labels have been created to serve communities as a platform where they can demonstrate their artistic visions and support each other's efforts. An example is the independent record label Ma Records in Prague, which emerged through an urge of young alumni of local jazz academies to present jazz music of the young generation. Similarly, the label Dur et Doux is a collective of musicians and a production structure. It includes about 30 professional musicians based between Lyon, the Loire, and the Ain, who are active in the Lyon scene of rock, jazz, and innovative music.

Export of a Local Scene Abroad Many independent record labels also try to expand to different territories. These labels often focus on niche genres or local music scenes and aim to promote their artists to a global audience. A good example of a label driven by this goal is Hevhetia, which has been focused on expanding its reach beyond Slovakia and promoting its music to a wider international audience. Similarly, the label We Jazz Records, based in Finland, is actively expanding its market in Germany, the UK, the U.S.A., and other territories.

Document and Preserve Jazz History Some independent jazz record labels may focus on reissuing rare or out-of-print jazz recordings from the past in order to preserve the history of the genre and make it more accessible to a new generation of listeners. One of the interviewed labels, Enja Records, is planning on reissuing albums from the catalog's history. Otherwise, there is no label interviewed for this book that is specifically focused on licensing and reprinting historical recordings. A good example of such a record label outside this study could be Craft Recordings, whose goal is to reissue influential jazz albums with the utmost reverence for the originals.

Support Avant-garde and Experimental Jazz Some independent jazz record labels may specialize in supporting more experimental or avant-garde forms of jazz, which may not receive as much attention from mainstream record labels. They may see their role as promoting boundary-pushing and innovative music. An example is one of our informants, Ma Records in Prague, or other independent enterprises such as Intakt Records based in Switzerland (1986) and French label RogueArt (2005). In the U.S.A., we can name, for example, Astral Spirits Records (2014), which is based in Texas, or New York-based labels Pi Recordings (2001) and Relative Pitch Records (2011).

Build a Loyal Fan Base Many independent jazz record labels aim to build a loyal fan base by developing a unique brand and curating a specific sound or aesthetic. They often prioritize fostering relationships with their listeners and creating a sense of community around their label. For instance, some labels focus on the analog format, recording and mixing music to analog tape and cutting directly to vinyl. These labels often have dedicated recording studios where live performances are recorded with minimal overdubs, reflecting production values reminiscent of earlier eras. This approach emphasizes authentic, high-quality recordings and exclusive releases, which helps in cultivating a dedicated and engaged community of listeners. For example, we can name the Berlin-based record label Low Swing, which focuses on the production of limited analog vinyl editions.

Financial Success While many independent jazz record labels are driven by a love of music and a desire to support jazz artists, some may also prioritize financial success. They may aim to sign commercially successful jazz musicians and release albums that have a broad appeal to jazz fans. However, it is challenging to prove this motive, as it is not something independent labels would typically admit about themselves since it goes against the ethos of the independent music scene. Nonetheless, it is essential to consider that there might be some micro-labels whose primary goal is to gain profit, despite the commonly held belief that their primary focus is on artistic integrity and supporting the jazz community.

Build an Alternative Income Channel or Provide a Platform for Another Enterprise/Event Another reason some labels are created is to build an alternative income channel or provide a platform for another enterprise or event. For example, Freifeld Tontraeger started as a platform for recordings created during a concert series. Similarly, We Jazz Records began as a club in 2009, initiated by a DJ who wanted to create new club nights spinning jazz records. Over time, We Jazz Records evolved into a company that produces events and offers PR services. It eventually launched a festival in Helsinki and, due to popular demand, transitioned into a record label. The founder's experience with other labels and encouragement from the local distribution network played a crucial role in this evolution. This example illustrates how some labels originate from broader initiatives and gradually expand to include a record label as part of their operations.

It's worth noting that the goals listed above are not mutually exclusive, and many independent jazz record labels may have a mix of different priorities. Additionally, the specific goals of a label may evolve over time as the label grows and changes. The author acknowledges that this list might not encompass all possible goals of jazz labels, but it serves as a representative overview of the interviewed labels.

3.2.2 Financial Strategies

> *"Digital and long tail royalties are the future (for the recording industry). And that should be the focus."*
>
> —Kervin M. Dockendorf (interview with the author, June 26, 2023)

While this statement from Kervin M. Dockendorf of Fangtasia Music underscores the industry's shift towards digital revenue streams, many independent jazz labels are reluctant to rely solely on digital music for their financial sustainability. Instead, these labels are exploring a variety of alternative products and innovative strategies to support their artists and maintain their operations. This chapter examines the creative approaches these labels are taking, from concert production and music licensing to crowdfunding and unique merchandising. By focusing on these diverse income channels, independent jazz labels are finding ways to thrive in an environment where digital royalties alone are often insufficient. Through a series of case studies, this chapter highlights the ingenuity and resilience of these labels as they adapt to the challenges of the modern music industry.

3.2.2.1 Income Channels

Jazz independent labels have long relied on a variety of financing models to sustain their businesses. With the rise of digital music streaming platforms, many independent jazz labels have had to get creative in order to continue operating. One of the most common financing models of the responding jazz independent labels is self-financing via multiple income channels, but the financial strategies vary for each informant. In addition to traditional physical products such as CDs, LPs, and merchandise, as well as digital formats like downloadable high-resolution files and streaming, most of the informants mentioned other income channels. These will be discussed in the following text based on the semi-structured interviews with jazz micro-label representatives (2021–2023).

Andreas Brandis shares a strategic approach to overcoming challenges in the music industry. Acknowledging the declining physical market and the limited profitability of vinyl due to high production costs, he emphasizes the need for a diversified business model. While digital channels partially fill the revenue gap, Brandis opts to expand into concert production through a booking agency, Tambour Management (changed to ACT Agency in 2023, and hereinafter referred to as ACT Agency). By curating and building unique concert formats, the agency not only broadens its creative scope but also establishes a symbiotic relationship with the label (interview with the author, May 13, 2022).

The ACT Agency started with artist management and booking, gradually evolving into a producer of curated concerts. Brandis emphasizes the importance of a diverse roster that spans classical to indie, showcasing the agency's versatility. This diversification allows them to offer a range of experiences to artists and collaborate creatively across genres. Despite facing challenges during the pandemic, the ACT Agency has grown to organize around 300 concerts annually, with a vision for further expansion (ibid.).

Addressing the financial aspect, Brandis discusses the integration of the agency and label turnovers. Initially, the label supported the agency's growth, but the goal is for the agency to become a significant contributor to the overall turnover. The synergy between the label and agency is highlighted, where different experiences come together to provide comprehensive support for artists (ibid.).

In terms of the label's historical revenue channels, Brandis mentions the enduring significance of international physical sales, indicating that digital sales are yet to reach parity. The label also engages in publishing, which predates its establishment and plays a crucial role, especially with neighboring rights.[1] Brandis clarifies that the publishing department operates as a separate entity, not directly contributing to the label's income (ibid.).

In a strategic diversification move, Heartcore Records is exploring the sale of digital education video products featuring one of its established artists. This innovative strategy seeks to capitalize on the artist's expertise and fan base by offering educational content that goes beyond traditional music releases. The digital education video products may encompass a range of topics, including guitar techniques, exercises, songwriting insights, and a close look into the artist's creative process. By venturing into the digital education space, Heartcore Records aims to not only generate additional revenue streams but also to cultivate a deeper connection between the artist and their audience. This strategy aligns with the label's commitment to adapt to evolving industry trends and provide unique value to fans while contributing to the overall sustainability of the label and its artists (interview with the author, January 9, 2023).

Besides that, Heartcore Records is exploring new avenues to bolster revenue and ensure the sustainability of its artists. In a strategic move, the label is considering collaboration with synchronizing supervisors to delve into the world of music licensing. Synchronization, or sync licensing, involves placing music in various media such as films, TV shows, commercials, and video games. This collaboration with synchronizing supervisors could open up opportunities for Heartcore Records and its artists to have their music featured in a range of visual content, expanding their reach and generating additional revenue (ibid.).

Crowdfunding has also become a popular financing option for jazz independent labels' projects. An example can be Heartcore Records' two crowdfunding campaigns organized between 2020 and 2023. This involves soliciting funding from fans and supporters through online platforms such as Kickstarter or Indiegogo or, in Heartcore Records' case, building the campaign independently on the label's website. Heartcore Records offered exclusive merchandise or limited edition releases as incentives for backers through their own website, which helped generate interest and increase funding (ibid.).

Kurt Rosenwinkel also mentioned a project where the distribution company provided a financial advance to the label. The advance had to be included in the distribution agreement and was recouped through the company's overall income in the following period (ibid.).

[1] "*Rights that are not directly connected with authors but with other parties in the creative process. They cover, for example, the rights of performers, recorded music companies, producers and broadcasters*" (Tschmuck, 2021, 221).

Grant opportunities are another financing option that is particularly prevalent in Europe for jazz independent labels. Various regional and national governments offer grants and funding programs to support the cultural sector, including jazz music. These grants can range from project-specific funding to general operating support for labels. Applying for grants can be a time-consuming process, but it can be a valuable source of funding for jazz labels that are committed to pursuing specific projects or expanding their operations. Some EU-based representatives mentioned that the grants are sometimes applied for by the artists themselves and often cover their own investment in their projects. This way, the artists can financially team up with the label without risking their own savings.

Hevhetia's financial system represents a unique blend of private and public support that has shaped the label's trajectory. Initially financed by a private noncultural company, the label found its footing through independent backing. However, Ján Súdzina, the owner, recognized the potential for broader cultural impact and sought additional support from the public sector. This shift allowed Hevhetia to expand its reach and contribute significantly to the cultural landscape. Despite initially relying on grants to bolster its endeavors, Ján Súdzina's vision for artistic freedom has led him to reconsider this approach. Cognizant of the limitations imposed by adapting projects to fund rules, he expressed a desire to discontinue the reliance on grants. This strategic decision reflects Hevhetia's commitment to preserving artistic autonomy and pushing creative boundaries beyond the constraints of traditional funding structures. To address the financial shortfall, Jan Súdzina is planning to reduce the investment allocated to productions (interview with the author, February 12, 2023).

Beyond record sales, Hevhetia demonstrates a multifaceted approach to building a global presence for the label and its artists. The emphasis on establishing a diverse portfolio involves strategic efforts to penetrate international markets, showcasing a commitment to reaching audiences globally. Hevhetia further expands its influence by organizing local and international festivals, fostering cultural traditions while concurrently broadening its network. The creation of an international exchange platform, JazzBus, serves as a dynamic hub for collaboration within the global jazz community, showcasing the label's dedication to fostering international connections. Additionally, Hevhetia sets itself apart by developing its own design and fashion brand, allowing the label to control the visual representation of its releases and reinforcing a distinctive aesthetic identity. This multifaceted strategy reflects Hevhetia's holistic vision for the label, intertwining artistic expression with a strategic global outlook and innovative branding initiatives (ibid.).

We Jazz Records adopts a multifaceted financial strategy that centers primarily on sales while also incorporating project-based funding to support specific projects. The label leverages funding for projects, such as PR campaigns in targeted regions like Germany, to enhance visibility and outreach. These strategic projects often involve hiring local PR teams and executing advertising campaigns. Label We Jazz Records actively pursues projects related to the export of their music, such as initiatives focused on the UK, U.S.A., and Germany. By exploring new ideas and establishing connections with different music scenes, the label continually seeks innovative ways to expand its reach and impact (interview with the author, April 19, 2022).

A noteworthy aspect of We Jazz Records' financial strategy is the incorporation of a magazine (We Jazz Magazine) which has gained prominence over its first three issues. The decision to transition the magazine to a quarterly publication with four issues annually indicates its growing importance within the overall financial structure of the label. This diversification into media, particularly the magazine, showcases an adaptability to changing industry dynamics and suggests that, in the eyes of the label manager Matti Nives, it could be considered a particularly viable and sustainable financial operation for We Jazz Records (ibid.).

Freifeld Tontraeger, under the leadership of Alexander Yannilos, has implemented a distinctive financial strategy that integrates label services as an extension of Yannilos' role as an audio engineer on album projects. By providing label services, Yannilos extends his involvement into various aspects of the music release process, including distribution, marketing, and promotion (interview with the author, April 26, 2022).

According to Vojta Drnek, Ma Records operates under a unique financial policy where the founders altruistically contribute their services without financial compensation. The ethos of the label centers on being a facilitator and support system for their musician friends, positioning themselves merely as a medium to help artists release their music. Ma Records prioritizes the artistic endeavor and the mutual passion for music. In this unconventional financial model, the founders offer their expertise, resources, and time on a voluntary basis, reinforcing a spirit of collaboration and camaraderie with the musicians they work with. By eliminating financial transactions and viewing themselves as a service-oriented platform, Ma Records fosters a community-driven approach that values artistic expression and the shared journey of bringing music to audiences (interview with the author, December 10, 2021).

In summary, the financial strategies of independent jazz micro-labels are characterized by their diversity and adaptability to the changing landscape of the music industry. As traditional revenue sources, such as physical sales, experienced a general decline after the year 2000, except for the slow growth after the year 2020 (IFPI, 2024), these labels have innovatively explored various income channels to sustain their operations and support their artists. Self-financing remains a cornerstone, with revenue generated from physical and digital formats, as well as other products. However, labels like ACT Music have expanded into concert production, creating events through their booking agency to supplement income. Similarly, Heartcore Records is leveraging crowdfunding to secure funding while exploring digital education products to diversify its revenue streams.

Grant opportunities, particularly prevalent in Europe, provide essential support for many labels, although some, like Hevhetia, are reconsidering this approach to maintain artistic freedom. Hevhetia's model exemplifies the integration of private and public support, expanding its influence through festivals, international platforms, and innovative branding. We Jazz Records has incorporated project-based funding and a quarterly magazine to enhance its visibility and financial stability.

Freifeld Tontraeger and Ma Records adopt more personalized and community-oriented financial strategies, focusing on collaborative support and voluntary contributions.

Overall, these varied approaches highlight the resilience and creativity of independent jazz labels in navigating the complexities of the modern music industry. By diversifying their income channels and leveraging both traditional and innovative funding models, they continue to promote and sustain the rich tradition of jazz music.

3.2.2.2 Label Deals

The changing landscape gave rise to the "360-degree deal," in which major labels began participating more extensively in all phases of an artist's career and in all income streams. This shift in the industry also witnessed the rise of independent producers and production companies, who gained significant influence, especially within the hip-hop genre and the advent of project studios (Hutchison et al., 2011, 217).

Independent labels often operate on a smaller scale with limited financial resources compared to major record labels. As a result, they may find it challenging to invest comprehensively in all aspects of an artist's career, as required by so-called "360-degree deals." Such agreements necessitate involvement in various revenue streams generated by the artist, including live performances, publishing, merchandise sales, endorsements, and other potential income sources (Cole, 2010). Artists may initially resist 360-degree deals, preferring separate agreements for distinct income streams. To address this resistance, labels are advised to present artists with choices, such as a 360-degree deal with a higher advance and commercial terms versus a "270-degree" deal covering recording and publishing only (Creative Law & Business, 2024).

The majority of informants do not partake in the artist's income beyond revenue generated from record sales. This traditional approach implies that labels typically limit their involvement to a share of the earnings, specifically from recorded music, refraining from participating in other revenue streams that artists may generate, such as live performances, merchandising, sponsorship deals, or endorsements.

One informant mentioned a scenario similar to a 360-degree deal involving a booking agency and its management division. ACT Music, extended its services to include ACT Agency, which handles bookings and artist management. This suggests that artists associated with ACT Agency might have an agreement where the agency receives a share of their earnings from various sources beyond typical music sales, live performances, and merchandise, similar to 360-degree deals in the entertainment industry. This, however, requires the sustainability of another team involved in the bookings, which is not always possible for developing micro-companies (interview with the author, May 13, 2022).

Razdaz Recordz, overseen by Ray Jafford, operates with a comprehensive strategy that revolves around a 360-degree deal to manage the multifaceted career of renowned bass player, composer, and singer Avishai Cohen. This integrated approach includes recording and licensing deals under one umbrella of Razdaz Recordz but leaves the artist's performing business as a separate entity, managed by Ray Jafford as well (interview with the author, September 22, 2021).

Werner Aldinger noted that Enja Records had previously handled publishing and booking activities, with specific team members assigned to execute these roles. However, as the team size reduced, the functionality of these departments became less central to the label's overall income (interview with the author, February 15, 2023).

In the diverse landscape of independent labels, deal structures exhibit considerable variation, and a distinctive arrangement involves a 50/50 split after recouping costs for both the musician and the label. This approach, however, is contingent upon the artist's career stage. Some representatives note that developing artists usually do not receive advance payments for creating a record. Instead, a prevalent practice involves labels receiving finished masters and initiating the recoupment process from the point immediately after the production concludes. In this scenario, costs incurred during manufacture, distribution, promotion, and other relevant expenses are recouped from the artist's earnings before profits are shared. This model reflects the pragmatic realities faced by developing artists and aligns with the label's strategy to mitigate financial risks while providing a platform for emerging talents to bring their music to the audience.

Micro-labels such as Ma Records set themselves apart by committing to providing 100 percent of the net revenues directly to the artists. Despite offering very basic services, the label prioritizes the artists' own ability to recoup their production costs by ensuring that the entirety of the revenue generated from music sales goes directly to those who create the music. This transparent, artist-centric approach aligns with Ma Records' philosophy of enabling musicians to share their work with the world without any financial barriers. Simultaneously, the label is not set to share any expenses with the artists and only contributes to the project with their own time and expertise (interview with the author, December 10, 2021).

The evolving music industry has seen the rise of the "360-degree deal," where major labels engage in all aspects of an artist's career, encompassing various income streams such as live performances, publishing, merchandise sales, and endorsements. This comprehensive involvement contrasts with independent labels, which often face financial constraints that limit their ability to invest extensively in artists' careers. Artists may resist 360-degree deals, preferring distinct agreements for different revenue sources, leading labels to offer alternatives like the "270-degree" deal. Some labels have limited their participation to revenue from record sales and some have adopted broader strategies, incorporating additional revenue sources despite fluctuations in their operational capacities. Independent jazz micro-labels exhibit diverse deal structures, from cost recoupment models to ensuring artists receive direct revenues, reflecting a pragmatic approach to financial risk and support for emerging talent. This variation underscores the industry's adaptive strategies to meet both economic realities and the needs of artists.

3.2.3 *Product Strategies*

In this chapter, we explore the product strategies employed by independent jazz record labels. We examine the various physical formats these labels offer, including vinyl and CDs. Additionally, we delve into their relationships with streaming services, analyzing how they approach digital formats. Furthermore, this chapter investigates the extended offerings beyond traditional music albums, such as exclusive merchandise, limited editions, and unique digital content, highlighting how these strategies enhance their overall product portfolio.

3.2.3.1 Physical Formats

Andreas Brandis: "*The international income on the physical side is still very important. So, we are still far away from the digital/physical 50:50 ratio. I mean, the market turned, and the ratio has been about 70 percent for physical speaking and 30 percent for digital speaking for the last year at ACT. So this year (2022) will probably be the first time that we will see something around 60:40, but still for physical*" (interview with the author, May 13, 2022).

According to this research, CD sales can still have a big impact on the revenue of independent jazz labels represented by the informants, despite the increasing popularity of digital downloads and streaming services. The reason might be the jazz enthusiasts and audiophiles who often place a high value on the sound quality and physical packaging of CDs. Some independent jazz labels invest heavily in high-quality recording equipment and packaging materials to create premium products for a developed artist with an established fan base.

All informants of this research manufacture or promote CD format on their label, and they claim that this type of product is a significant source of their income. This does not apply to Enja Records, with more than 800 titles in the catalog, for which there is a significantly higher income from digital sales of the entire catalog (interview with the author, February 15, 2023).

According to some informants, the most effective is to sell physical records at the event of the artist/s. Some labels use this opportunity to provide the physical records to the artist at no cost and have the artist recoup their investment through direct sales. Those labels that cover the full costs of the album can offer the artists their own product for purchase.

For Aldringer, CD sales are also important for independent jazz labels because they provide a reliable source of revenue. While digital downloads and streaming services can generate revenue for labels and artists, they are often subject to fluctuations in streaming rates and changes in algorithms. By contrast, CD sales provide a more predictable and steady stream of revenue that can help independent labels maintain financial stability. He also points out that the physical medium is what makes the album relevant: "*…if I do only digital, it's very hard to get attention,*" he says (interview with the author, February 15, 2023).

Dave Douglas, representing Greenleaf Music, shares a similar perspective on the evolving landscape of music releases. He explores the possibility of shifting towards digital-only releases as a means to sign more artists and streamline the label's operations. However, he candidly reveals the resistance encountered when proposing this idea to artists, as there remains a prevailing desire for physical formats like CDs or vinyl. Douglas attributes this preference to a mental aspect but also recognizes the influence of a generation, including critics, who still rely on tangible formats for their appreciation of music. Despite the potential advantages of digital-only releases, Douglas acknowledges the enduring importance of CDs in the promotional realm. His reflections shed light on the challenges and complexities that labels face in adapting to changing industry norms and preferences. Ultimately, the label continues to produce CDs to align with the prevailing expectations and promotional requirements within the music industry (interview with the author, February 23, 2023).

Even though the overall sales of the physical product are decreasing, CD sales remain an important part of the revenue stream, and many independent jazz labels continue to prioritize the production and distribution of high-quality CDs for jazz enthusiasts and collectors.

In the last decade, vinyl LPs have come back into the music market, with sales steadily increasing yearly. A growing interest in vinyl has partly driven this resurgence as a physical and collectible format and nostalgia for the classic sound and feel of vinyl records has become a "new" industry standard. For jazz labels, in particular, vinyl LPs have become an important format for both new releases and reissues of classic albums. Jazz enthusiasts and collectors often value the sound quality and packaging of vinyl records, which can provide a richer and more immersive listening experience than digital formats (Sax, 2016).

Independent jazz labels have also recognized the sales of vinyl LPs as a revenue source. However, several factors have significantly increased vinyl LP manufacturing costs at the beginning of 2021. One major factor is the global pandemic, which has disrupted supply chains and caused shortages of raw materials, including vinyl. As a result, vinyl manufacturers have had to pay higher prices for vinyl pellets, the raw material used to make records. In addition to higher raw material costs, vinyl pressing plants have also faced increased demand for their services as vinyl sales have surged in recent years. This has led to longer lead times for pressing orders and higher prices for manufacturing service prices as pressing plants seek to manage their workload and prioritize high-volume customers. Finally, labor costs have also contributed to the rising cost of vinyl LP manufacture. All of these factors have contributed to significant price increases for vinyl LP manufacture in the last 2 years, with some estimates suggesting that the cost of pressing a single record has increased by as much as 50 percent in some cases. These higher costs have impacted not only independent labels and artists but also major labels, who have faced supply chain disruptions and delays due to the pandemic. As a result, the cost of vinyl records has increased for consumers, and the industry as a whole is grappling with how to manage these rising costs while continuing to meet the demand for vinyl LPs (iMusician, 2021).

Andreas Brandis: *"…vinyl is nice to have and is asked for by the artists and also by customers, but the profit margin is very small because the production costs are so high, and the production lead times are insane at the moment due to a crisis of raw material, et cetera. So that's not the solution. You can see the hype around vinyl at the moment, but it's not a sustainable solution"* (interview with the author, May 13, 2022).

Despite the complications related to LP production, most of the informants in this book have some vinyl LP products in their catalogs. However, it is usually a subject for consideration whether the project promises effective recoupment or whether there is financial support that can protect the label from risks of loss in case the demanding product does not meet the sales expectations.

One of the informants, Matti Nives from We Jazz Records, differs from his peers in that he focuses on vinyl singles. While most jazz labels primarily release full-length albums, We Jazz Records has made a name for itself by producing a series of 7-inch vinyl singles featuring exclusive tracks from its catalog. According to Matti Nives, this format is very popular among his customers and generates interesting revenue for the company and the artists (interview with the author, April 19, 2022).

Matti Nives: *"The format sales depend on from album to album. (…) Vinyl is really expensive to make, [and] the margin is super thin, but I still think that it is kind of the best format for many of our albums. I would say vinyl is still the biggest part of our income because there's a scene for it, and we're so much identifying with that scene…So I think people also expect that from us. There have been some seven-inch single releases that have been really successful"* (ibid.).

The attitude of Werner Aldinger from Enja Records is more directly focused on the CD format: *"With CDs, the span of what you earn is much bigger than with vinyl. Because vinyl's really expensive, and most of the time, you just recoup the costs of the manufacturing. It's great to have vinyl, but you don't really make money on that. Whereas CDs, okay, let's say the sales are still going down, but it's still another percentage of what you earn by selling them. I think in other genres, it's different. But in the jazz community, it's still important to have the CDs*" (interview with the author, February 15, 2023).

Similarly, Ján Súdzina considers the CD format to be the key product for the label: *"The most income is from CDs and vinyls, of course, mostly CDs, because that's where the ratio is. And the CD also works as a promotional tool*" (interview with the author, February 12, 2023).

Ray Jafford from Razdaz Recordz also acknowledges the importance of CD sales, but he gives an example of a special occasion when an LP project secured more profit than any other CD production: *"The best selling physical product is CD. But here is an another example: we did this special LP box set, we printed two thousand two hundred units, and we have about five hundred left. That's pretty good bearing in mind where we have been dealing with covid pandemic. (…) When you think there are six vinyls in the box, that's a lot of vinyls; it's ten thousand vinyls. So look at that as one product right now; it hasn't even been out a year yet, and it's already done ten thousand vinyls. So, in this case, I would say vinyl sales would be higher than CD sales. Our digital income although it's substantially heavy in certain territories and especially in certain titles, but it's not reaching those income levels. Because the income from streams is so small for such a volume. I mean, you have to do a hundred million (streams) to start thinking about real income*" (interview with the author, September 22, 2021).

Some independent record labels care about the ecological aspect of their businesses and are taking steps to reduce their environmental impact. Enterprises that care about the ecological aspect of their businesses may take this into consideration when choosing a manufacturer. They may look for manufacturers that prioritize sustainability and use environmentally friendly materials and processes in their production, or they may choose to work with manufacturers that are located closer to their distribution centers or customers in order to reduce transportation emissions and overall carbon footprint. Matti Nives says, "The *World, the planet that we live on, that's the ultimate Limited Edition*" (interview with the author, April 19, 2022).

3.2.3.2 Digital Formats

Independent jazz labels use a variety of channels to sell digital music, from their own websites and online stores to third-party retailers and streaming platforms.

Since the inception of Spotify in 2006, a notable divide has existed within the music industry over its treatment of artists' royalties. Many major artists and independent record labels initially resisted the idea of releasing their music on streaming platforms due to perceived inequities. Among those who vocally criticized the service, Taylor Swift and Thom Yorke were prominent figures, expressing their concerns about the platform's compensation structure. However, the landscape began to shift over time, and both these artists ultimately appeared on streaming services (Luckerson, 2016).

Although these artists and many other independent artists decided to let their music be streamed, there still are some major celebrities who have not allowed it up to now (2023). Notably, Garth Brooks and Joanna Newsom are still missing from Spotify, with Brooks holding an exclusive deal with Amazon Music and Newsom's primary catalog remaining unavailable on the platform, underscoring the continued complexities and challenges surrounding digital music distribution (Whines, 2023).

Some independent jazz micro-labels have also avoided uploading their catalog to streaming services due to concerns about the services' policies and practices. One of the main concerns for these labels was the low royalty rate that streaming services offer to artists and labels. While major labels may be able to negotiate more favorable terms, independent labels often receive only a small fraction of the revenue generated by streams of their music. Another concern is the lack of transparency around how streaming services calculate and report royalties. Independent labels may be wary of entering into agreements with streaming services without a clear understanding of how their music will be monetized and how they will be compensated (Smith & Telang, 2017).

As a result, some independent jazz micro-labels have chosen either to avoid uploading their catalog to streaming services altogether, or looked for other methods, such as delaying the release of the album in the streamed format. Instead, they focused on selling physical copies of their music and making it available through other digital channels. By taking this approach, these labels were able to maintain more control over how their music is distributed and monetized.

In the following text, the author researches the labels' past and current approaches to streaming service distribution and related strategies.

Was there ever a point when you refused to publish something on streaming services when they started?

Andreas Brandis: "*Earlier in life i worked for ECM at Universal, and ECM refused to stream completely at the beginning. When I came to ACT (ACT Music), ACT did not refuse to stream, but there was a windowing [strategy]. So the digital release always took place like three months after the physical one. Still, the team was convinced that it would have an impact to give the physical products a focus for a certain period of time and then release them digitally for the world. Of course, excluding downloads. So, a release was always in physical CD plus downloads, and streaming was windowed about three months after the physical release. And we changed that only at the end of 2016 or the beginning of 2017. So, we kept that quiet for a while*" (interview with the author, May 13, 2022).

What made you change your mind?

"*The pressure increased because more and more territories asked for it. So every year when I was visiting our artists, especially in the Nordic countries, they complained that if something's not on Spotify, in Sweden, for example, it does not exist. So for them, Spotify was a very important marketing platform, rather than a pure streaming platform, and of course, also the artists from certain territories complained that they were not visible and 'people wonder'...So, it was a long discussion. And, of course, digital downloads started their way down the drain. I'd say in 2015, digital downloads still had quite an importance in the digital turnover, and that changed with a high tempo over the years. So when this was marginalized, we decided now we have to sync everything, and I think, in the end, it was a good decision, and we could see an increase in digital turnover.*" (interview with the author, May 13, 2022).

In recent years, there has been a shift in attitudes toward streaming services among independent jazz labels. Many labels have recognized the importance of making their music available on popular streaming platforms to reach a wider audience and generate more revenue.

One factor that has contributed to this shift is the growing popularity of jazz among younger listeners, many of whom primarily consume music through streaming services. By making their music available on these platforms, independent jazz labels can connect with a new generation of fans and grow their audience. Another factor is the changing economics of the music industry. With the decline of physical music sales and the rise of streaming, many independent labels have found that they need to embrace new distribution channels in order to survive and thrive in a digital-first landscape.

As a result, the interviewed independent jazz labels have now made their catalogs available on streaming services like Spotify, Apple Music, and Tidal. While there are still concerns about royalty rates and transparency, these labels recognize that streaming services are an important part of the music ecosystem and that they need to be a part of it in order to succeed.

Matti Nives embraces the access to the extensive music libraries on streaming services from the listeners' perspective: "*There's nothing to romanticize about the lack of access*" (interview with the author, April 19, 2022).

Werner Aldinger acknowledges the importance of the digital format but sees the work related to the digital album as "not the most fun" and points out that the production process and the tangibility of the LP product have a special feeling to it: "*The digital part is the most important. It's not the most fun. It's more fun to do vinyl, for example. I just got a vinyl of a new production this morning. That's very nice because you can hold it in your hands and it feels great. With digital products, you don't have any cost (for manufacture), you upload it, and then you don't have to do anything. So, of course, digital is especially important if you have a huge catalog like we do because we have, let's say, around 800 active titles*" (interview with the author, February 15, 2023).

The digital product strategy of some of the informants is to provide high-fidelity masters that can help to establish their brand and reputation as a purveyor of quality jazz music. Fans who appreciate the subtleties of jazz music are often willing to pay a premium for high-quality recordings, and labels that can provide these recordings are more likely to attract and retain loyal fans.

Alexander Yannilos: "*There is a difference between an mp3 from Spotify and a high-resolution file.*[2] *It is the idea of downloading an uncompromised and uncompressed file instead of streaming it. I like that I can put the artwork into the zip file as well. And it can vary. So maybe there is a poster or video file included in the download. It can be pictures of the actual recording. So I like the idea of adding things to the standard repertoire and also having just digital downloads that contain more than just the audio but are completely non-physical at the same time*" (interview with the author, April 26, 2022).

Jan Súdzina's label, Hevhetia, has adopted a flexible policy that respects the wishes of artists who prefer not to have their music placed on streaming services. This approach reflects a commitment to accommodating the diverse preferences of the label's roster of artists. Hevhetia recognizes that some artists may have specific reservations or concerns about the impact of streaming platforms on their work, whether related to financial considerations, artistic control, or other factors (interview with the author, February 12, 2023).

While most labels recognize streaming as an essential channel for distributing their music, their acceptance is more pragmatic than enthusiastic. Although they acknowledge the necessity of having a presence on streaming platforms, these

[2] Spotify announced its HiFi tier in February 2021, promising CD-quality, lossless audio for Premium subscribers (Spotify 2021). Despite delays, recent leaks (2024) suggest its imminent release, supporting up to 2117 kbps and 24-bit/44.1 kHz audio in FLAC format. This aims to compete with Apple Music and Amazon Music, which already offer lossless audio at no extra cost (Weatherbed, 2024).

labels often refrain from developing comprehensive strategies specifically tailored to the streaming ecosystem. Instead, they maintain a cautious approach, prioritizing traditional and tangible formats while using streaming services primarily as a supplementary distribution method. This cautious acceptance reflects a broader trend among independent jazz labels, balancing the demands of modern digital consumption with their commitment to more traditional music formats.

3.2.3.3 Extended Sortiment

Charts

In addition to the traditional avenues of physical and digital music media, some record labels have expanded their offerings to include the sale of music charts in both physical and digital formats. An exemplary case in point is Razdaz Recordz, Greenleaf Records, and ACT Music, which provide audiences with tangible and digital representations of music charts (interviews with the author, 2021–2023).

Similarly, Heartcore Records has embraced the trend of selling digital music charts, acknowledging the contemporary shift in music consumption habits. Currently focusing on the digital realm, the label is strategically planning to extend its offerings by venturing into the production and release of a physical book containing music charts (interview with the author, January 9, 2023).

Video Products

Heartcore Records has strategically diversified its portfolio by releasing multiple music masterclasses conducted by the renowned guitarist Kurt Rosenwinkel. These video products have emerged as essential components of the label's business strategy, adding educational content and involving the visual dimension to the traditional auditory experience. By providing consumers with in-depth insights into the artistic process and techniques of an accomplished musician, such video products not only contribute to the label's revenue stream but also enhance its brand image as a comprehensive platform for music education and appreciation (ibid.).

Merchandising

Jazz independent labels, such as Heartcore Records, We Jazz Records, Greenleaf, and ACT Music, have strategically incorporated merchandise sales into their business model. Heartcore Records currently offers T-shirts and tote bags, with plans to expand its merchandise range through on-demand suppliers. We Jazz Records provides a selection of items, including beanies, ball caps, sweatshirts, and tote bags in the past, relating the branding of the merchandise to a specific project or product. Greenleaf has introduced tote bags and ball caps with the company's logo to its merchandise lineup. ACT Music stands out with an extensive range, including jackets, beanies, t-shirts, slip mats for turntables, and tote bags with the company's logo (interviews with the author, 2021–2023).

3.2.3.4 Repertoire

Digital distribution has significantly influenced various aspects of artistic production, including the length and volume of tracks, as well as genre crossover. The insights from several industry professionals illustrate these changes and their impacts.

Andreas Brandis notes a significant shift towards singles, driven by the rise of streaming services. In the past, jazz singles were almost unheard of, but now they form a crucial part of their release strategy, necessitating extensive content creation. The role of content has expanded dramatically, with a need for dynamic, attention-grabbing materials such as short videos and reels to keep up with today's fast-paced media environment. This shift has also transformed roles within the label, emphasizing content creation and management. Brandis also discusses the value of collaborations, stressing that they must be authentic and musically meaningful rather than superficial attempts to boost visibility through algorithms (interview with the author, May 13, 2022).

Dave Douglas appreciates the flexibility that digital distribution offers, allowing him to release music of any length and in various formats. This adaptability enables him to cater to different audiences and projects, including exclusive subscriber albums on Bandcamp and extensive live recordings. Such releases would have been unfeasible in the pre-digital era, highlighting the new possibilities afforded by modern distribution methods (interview with the author, February 23, 2023).

Alexander Yannilos emphasizes the importance of innovation and progressiveness in music. His label, often associated with jazz, embraces a wide range of genres, including electronic and experimental music. Yannilos is cautious about labeling his music strictly as jazz to avoid limiting perceptions, striving instead for a broad and inclusive approach that champions a progressive attitude towards music (interview with the author, April 26, 2022).

Werner Aldinger highlights that his catalog includes a variety of genres beyond jazz. This diversification is not a commercial strategy but an organic decision driven by the artists themselves. His musical journey, which began with playing in rock and world music bands, reflects the natural evolution of his interests and the ever-changing music scene. However, marketing eclectic and innovative music poses unique challenges. While traditional jazz might be easier to sell, music that defies categorization often proves more difficult to market effectively (interview with the author, February 15, 2023).

Heartcore Records has featured multiple artists across various genres on their albums, including a notable collaboration with Eric Clapton, which significantly boosted the album's performance on streaming services. However, this outcome was not the result of a deliberate strategy by the label but rather arose from the artist's circumstances and an organic collaboration (interview with the author, January 9, 2023).

None of the interviewed labels identified the strategy of featuring artists on albums to increase streaming numbers. According to the labels, such collaborations are driven primarily by artistic motivations. Nevertheless, these instances have proven beneficial, as they attract new audiences and potentially enhance streaming revenue for the labels.

3.2.4 Distribution Strategies

3.2.4.1 Physical Distribution

Maintaining the physical distribution of independent jazz micro-labels involves a combination of strategic partnerships, direct sales, and relationship building. By effectively leveraging these channels, independent jazz micro-labels can reach a wider audience and build a sustainable business model. Independent jazz labels typically maintain physical distribution through a variety of channels, including direct sales, partnerships with distributors on a contractual basis, and relationships with record stores.

One common strategy is to sell albums directly through the label's website or online store. This approach allows the label to retain control over the entire sales process and maintain a direct relationship with its customers. Another option is to partner with distributors who specialize in physical distribution. These distributors can help the label get its music into retail stores and other outlets. They may also provide services like warehousing and shipping, making it easier for the label to manage inventory and logistics. What has demonstrated considerable efficacy are the tour sales, with artists actively engaging in the direct sale of their products at merchandise tables during performances.

Partnering with Major and/or Independent Distributors
Several record labels featured in the interviews have adopted a diversified approach to distribution, collaborating with multiple channels to navigate the complexities of physical sales. This not only showcased flexibility but also leveraged the strengths of different distributors for global reach. These examples demonstrate the importance of tailored strategies, whether through individual partnerships or collaboration with larger entities and their sub-distributors, showcasing the adaptability of record labels in optimizing their reach and impact.

Werner Aldinger reflects on the evolving landscape of distribution, noting a substantial reduction in the number of distributors compared to two decades ago. He describes a significant shift in their global distribution network, emphasizing that the expansive reach they once had in countries like Egypt and Argentina is no longer feasible. The current distribution strategy focuses on key regions, with distributors like Edel in Germany, Proper in England, Ultra-Vybe, Inc. in Japan, or Naxos in the U.S.A. The informant acknowledges the organic nature of this reduction, attributing it to the changing dynamics within the industry. His insight emphasizes the need for adaptability in the face of shifting industry dynamics, especially in regions where physical distribution is waning (interview with the author, February 15, 2023).

Andreas Brandis discusses his perspective on the future of physical distribution for ACT Music. He envisions a shift towards more streamlined strategies, possibly handling distribution themselves in the coming years, eliminating the need for physical distributors in every country. The idea is to have a central entity taking care of global distribution or directly delivering to major shops. In line with this, ACT Music is developing a new website and webshop system to allow customers to buy directly from the producer, akin to the trend in agriculture where consumers prefer purchasing produce directly from the source (interview with the author, May 13, 2022).

Regarding direct-to-fan (hereinafter referred to as D2F) services, Brandis mentions that ACT Music can ship worldwide, but for some territories, it may not be cost-effective for customers due to shipping expenses. ACT's web shop is managed by a third party for financial transactions, and they collaborate with their manufacturer, Optimal, to ship from their own warehouse. Notably, they are exploring innovative solutions like delivering physical products to Bandcamp through their distributor in the U.S. This move is seen as a strategic and convenient sales platform for the U.S.-based customers, offering faster and more cost-effective shipping options (ibid.).

He points out the challenges of traditional chains like Barnes and Noble, which often prioritize mainstream top-sellers, making it difficult for independent, instrumental content. In contrast, he mentioned Bandcamp, which offers an attractive alternative with a well-established platform and a community of artists, providing a significant traffic boost. Despite uncertainties about Bandcamp's future trajectory post-acquisition, Brandis sees it as a valuable solution for independent labels like ACT Music, addressing the unique challenges of placing instrumental music in mainstream outlets (ibid.).

Heartcore Records embarked on its business journey by exclusively selling D2F units through its website. After 3 years of substantial catalog growth, the decision was made to expand distribution channels, leading to a collaboration with the independent U.S.-based distributor Red Eye Worldwide. This strategic partnership enabled wider market access. Subsequently, after another 3 years, Heartcore Records shifted to The Orchard, aiming to tap into a more targeted jazz audience through a distributor with major label coverage in all territories. Moreover, the label has extended its global reach through a distinct collaboration in Japan. Here, Heartcore Records independently distributes its catalog via Ultra-Vybe, Inc., a partnership that involves the manufacturing of translated versions of its records within the Japanese territory (interview with the author, January 9, 2023).

Despite these developments, the D2F model remains integral, and the website remains active. Moreover, in early 2023, the label ventured into the Bandcamp platform, establishing a dedicated store to connect with customers familiar with the platform and actively participate in the community it aims to support. To enhance customer engagement, Heartcore Records established a partnership with 8merch D2F service in Poland and the U.S.A., facilitating the fulfillment of orders placed at the label's website and their Bandcamp page (ibid.).

Razdaz's Ray Jafford highlights a significant shift in their distribution strategy, transitioning from Alternative Distribution Alliance[3] (hereinafter referred to as ADA) to Believe/naïve. ADA served as their major distributor, excluding Israel and the U.S.A. However, the move to Believe/naïve involved a strategic restructuring, with Believe/naïve taking over distribution in Israel, the U.S.A., and globally. This reorganization involved Believe handling the digital side and naïve managing the physical distribution, which, though smaller, is still a crucial aspect of their business. The decision to align with Believe stemmed from their robust capabilities in the digital realm, showcasing a clear focus on the evolving landscape of music distribution. The transition was further motivated by the conclusion of the agreement with ADA. This strategic move not only consolidated their distribution under Believe/naïve but also streamlined their reporting process, with a unified report encompassing all their numbers annually (interview with the author, September 22, 2021).

Greenleaf Music's Dave Douglas discusses their long-term engagement in selling CDs, emphasizing their distributor, Red Eye Worldwide's, significant role in CD sales for their music. Despite not delving too deeply into where these CDs are sold, they express awareness of the decline of traditional outlets like Tower Records, relying on alternative avenues. The interviewee notes the continued demand for CDs, with people purchasing directly from the artist through platforms like Bandcamp. They highlight Red Eye's seamless integration with Bandcamp's direct-to-fan model, recognizing it as a strength in their distribution strategy. However, the interviewee acknowledges a shift in focus within the streaming landscape, where there is a growing insistence on presenting the full project. Despite the evolving dynamics, the artist remains active in exploring all possible channels to cater to diverse consumer preferences and distribution models (interview with the author, February 23, 2023).

Matti Nives shares the inception story of their record store in 2019, sparked by the acquisition of a vast jazz record collection from Switzerland. The shop, based in Finland, showcases a diverse array of music genres, including their label, We Jazz Records, alongside used and new records. The distribution strategy involves handling orders in Finland while relying on Kudos distribution for global reach, with sub-distributors like Groove Attack in Germany. The challenges posed by Brexit led to innovative solutions, such as utilizing sub-distributors to navigate complexities in sending records to different countries. Nives emphasizes the significance of the German market, the largest outside of Finland, and discusses the evolving landscape post-Brexit. We Jazz Records actively collaborates with Bandcamp, which serves as a pivotal platform that has contributed significantly to the label's current position (interview with the author, April 19, 2022).

In addition to the distribution channels mentioned above, some independent jazz labels also choose to ship their products personally through the post office or other

[3] ADA—Alternative Distribution Alliance—is a music distribution company owned by Warner Music Group, which represents the rights to various independent record labels.

shipping services. This approach can be particularly effective for micro-labels with a small operation or those with a strong DIY ethos. By handling shipping and fulfillment in-house, these labels can maintain complete control over the process and ensure that their products are packaged and shipped with special care. In some cases, label representatives may even include handwritten notes or other personalized touches to help build relationships with their customers. However, this approach can also be time-consuming and resource-intensive.

Alexander Yannilos maintains relationships with local stores and suggests his artists bring their products to particular retail stores themselves. He reflects on the tangible impacts of physical store closures, like the EMI music store in Vienna, highlighting the personal touch needed for sustaining physical distribution networks. Shipping CDs from their online shop involves his personal effort, filling out forms and sending out orders worldwide, maintaining a personal touch with customers. Despite the workload, the informant values the personal connection, highlighting the difference between a commercial label and one driven by artistic output and personal engagement with both the music and its audience (interview with the author, April 26, 2022).

Vojta Drnek explains Ma Records' approach to physical product distribution exclusively through Bandcamp. The label forwards orders directly to artists, eliminating the need for central catalog storage and supporting the label's low-cost structure (interview with the author, December 10, 2021).

3.2.4.2 Merch Table

The presence of a merch table and the sale of physical formats at events hold significant value for independent jazz micro-labels. Ray Jafford, representing Razdaz Recordz, underscores the importance of selling physical units, such as CDs and LPs, directly to fans during Avishai Cohen concerts. This strategy not only boosts immediate cash flow but also strengthens the connection between the artist and the audience. Jafford notes that territories like the U.S.A., France, and parts of Europe still show strong demand for physical products, making event sales a crucial component of their overall sales strategy. He highlights that live shows provide an essential revenue stream, claiming that maintaining a physical presence and engaging directly with show-goers can lead to substantial sales, enhancing the financial health of the label and the artist (interview with the author, September 22, 2021).

Douglas also highlights the critical role of selling CDs at live events for both artists and the label. Representing Greenleaf Music, he emphasizes that direct sales at concerts and gigs are vital for fostering a strong connection between artists and their audiences. These in-person interactions not only enhance the fan experience but also drive sales, as attendees are more likely to purchase CDs and return for future performances. Douglas underscores the consistency of this practice throughout his career, noting that the people who attend shows are the most invested in the music and, thus, the most likely to support the artist through physical purchases. This approach ensures that CD sales remain a significant and effective component of Greenleaf Music's overall strategy (interview with the author, February 23, 2023).

Kurt Rosenwinkel from Heartcore Records shares his positive experiences with selling physical albums and merchandise while on tour. He highlights the significant benefits of offering fans the opportunity to purchase signed products and meet the artist in person (interview with the author, January 9, 2023). This interaction not only adds a personal touch and unique value to the products but also fosters a deeper connection between the artist and their audience.

3.2.4.3 Digital Distribution

Navigating the transition from physical to digital distribution has been a significant journey for many older record labels, marking a transformative era in the music industry. In a revealing interview with Werner Aldinger from Enja Records, the challenges and evolution of this process are discussed. When digital distribution first emerged, the landscape was notably different. Back then, the label relied on external distributing entities, such as Edel, to manage the intricate process of uploading files and handling metadata, given the extensive catalog already in existence. Over time, as technology and industry dynamics shifted, the label transitioned to taking a more hands-on approach, personally managing file uploads and distribution processes. This shift, while empowering, also brought to light past errors in the metadata handled by external entities. The interview further explores distributor changes, illustrating the challenges and disruptions that can arise, shedding light on the complexities faced by older labels adapting to the digital environment (interview with the author, February 15, 2023).

ACT's Andreas Brandis delves into the complexities of music distribution in the digital age, where the dynamics between physical and digital realms create challenges. He points out that promotional efforts by local physical distributors are often impacted by digital platforms, like Spotify, where listeners might discover new music. However, Brandis highlights the intricate technical challenges of managing digital distribution territory by territory. Sending metadata to multiple distributors and dealing with the ensuing administrative tasks can be overwhelming. He explains the difficulties when platforms like Spotify assess new releases from an international perspective, creating potential conflicts in promotional efforts (interview with the author, May 13, 2022).

To navigate these challenges, Brandis reveals a common strategy adopted by many labels and artists globally. Instead of dealing with the complexities of individual distributors, they often opt for a single global distributor. In Brandis' case, Kontor New Media, based in Hamburg, serves as their main digital distributor, handling digital distribution, promotion, and engagement across various platforms. This approach allows for a more streamlined and efficient management of digital distribution efforts. Brandis notes that such distributors operate on a global scale, comparable to industry leaders like The Orchard, providing a comprehensive solution to the evolving complexities of digital distribution (ibid.).

Since aligning with Believe's distribution, Razdaz Recordz has strategically invested in optimizing its presence on YouTube, making substantial efforts and financial commitments to refine and enhance its content. This proactive approach involved cleaning up and organizing platforms, ensuring that the released content of their main artist not only garnered visibility but also received prominent placement on hotlists, attracting more views. The significant investment made by Razdaz Recordz during this period underscored the label's commitment to maximizing the impact of its music on digital platforms (interview with the author, September 22, 2021).

Ma Records and Freifeld Tontraeger, two smaller local record labels, have embraced the digital landscape by utilizing digital aggregators for their distribution needs. Ma Records has opted for Amuse (interview with the author, December 10, 2021), and Freifeld Tontraeger has chosen CD Baby as its digital aggregator of choice (interview with the author, April 26, 2022). Both labels have seamlessly integrated digital files into their distribution strategies, allowing audiences to access and download their albums in high resolution through their website or through platforms such as Bandcamp. This strategic use of digital aggregators and distribution channels reflects a low-cost approach by labels with a smaller financial capital.

While digitally distributing via contracted distributor Red Eye Worldwide, Dave Douglas emphasizes the significant role Bandcamp plays in his label, Greenleaf Music. He views Bandcamp as the best argument against Spotify's policy, appreciating its supportive community and effective D2F sales model. Their transition to Bandcamp occurred when they introduced Bandcamp for labels, which took over the storefront responsibilities from Greenleaf Music, streamlining operations and allowing the label to focus more on creativity and less on logistics. Douglas values Bandcamp's ability to offer subscriptions, which had been part of Greenleaf's model since its inception but were much harder to manage independently. The sense of community and the platform's comprehensive features make Bandcamp an ideal partner for Greenleaf Music's digital distribution strategy (interview with the author, February 23, 2023).

Dave Douglas highlights the importance of Bandcamp's subscription model for Greenleaf Music, emphasizing its role in providing financial support and fostering a community around their music. The subscription is an annual fee that gives subscribers access to the entire catalog, allowing them to stream and download all available music. Subscribers also receive early notices about new releases, and those at higher tiers get free new releases as part of their membership. Douglas appreciates the ease of managing subscriptions through Bandcamp, which has streamlined their operations significantly by handling storefront responsibilities and integrating with their existing distribution model (ibid.).

Heartcore Records recently decided to switch its distributor to The Orchard, aiming to enhance its digital distribution efforts and secure better placements in playlists. This change was driven by a desire to reach a wider audience, particularly within the jazz genre, and to benefit from The Orchard's expertise, network, and active involvement in digital platforms. The decision was influenced by a personal connection with an enthusiastic representative of The Orchard and the potential advantages of having a local presence in Hamburg, Germany. With this new partnership, Heartcore Records hopes to achieve greater visibility and engagement for their artists in the digital landscape, leveraging The Orchard's capabilities to maximize their online impact. Additionally, Heartcore Records has mirrored their entire catalog on Bandcamp, further extending their digital reach, and is also selling WAV files directly through their website, ensuring high-quality audio options for their fans (interview with the author, January 9, 2023).

Razdaz Recordz recently switched its distributor to Believe, seeking to improve its digital distribution and gain better placements in playlists. This decision was made to leverage Believe's advanced digital marketing strategies and extensive reach within the music-streaming ecosystem. By partnering with Believe, Razdaz Recordz aims to increase its visibility and connect more effectively with its audience online (interview with the author, September 22, 2021).

In the evolving landscape of music distribution, some labels are actively searching for better digital distribution partners to enhance their online presence and streaming performance. Meanwhile, others are focusing on building a strong community within platforms like Bandcamp and are less concerned with expanding their footprint on streaming services. Some labels try to combine both efforts to increase profit and help their sustainability.

3.2.5 Marketing Strategies

In an ever-evolving music industry, marketing strategies are pivotal for the success of artists and labels alike. This chapter delves into the diverse approaches adopted by interviewed record labels to navigate both digital and partly physical landscapes. The semi-structured interviews with the informants didn't include a specific section concerning the retail marketing of physical products. The author chose this approach to emphasize the increasing importance of digital marketing strategies, as digital sales are growing rapidly and have become a substantial part of the music industry income (IFPI, 2024). However, this does not mean that physical product marketing is entirely disregarded. In fact, the recent rise in physical music sales highlights its continuing importance (ibid.). Several informants mentioned that they outsource this aspect through their contractual distributors, indicating that while digital marketing is prioritized, physical product marketing remains a crucial component for many labels within the industry.

3.2.5.1 Marketing on Streaming Platforms

As the music industry undergoes transformative shifts, some independent jazz micro-labels with contractually involved distributors are intensifying their efforts to develop tailored strategies, while others using aggregators face distinct challenges, such as limited time capacities and constrained access to pitching systems. These differing approaches underscore the evolving nature of the industry and the need for nuanced strategies to thrive in the dynamic world of streaming.

Andreas Brandis from ACT Music sheds light on the collaborative efforts with their distributor, Kontor New Media, emphasizing their active involvement in label development. Kontor New Media takes charge of pitching, playlisting, sales marketing, and promotional campaigns, extending their reach to platforms like Deezer and Gobuz. Brandis acknowledges the complexity of the setup, with geographical considerations influencing the effectiveness of teams in different regions. Notably, in cases where a release has a strong French focus, Andreas opts to give it to the "French team" (ACT Music's French sub-distributor), bypassing the content from Kontor New Media for that territory. This strategic approach aims to leverage the local team's stronger connections with French curators, illustrating the nuanced decision-making involved in optimizing the collaboration for the best results (interview with the author, May 13, 2022).

Brandis reveals a notable shift in strategy, highlighting that prior to the streaming era, ACT Music never worked with singles. The traditional concept of singles, primarily associated with radio play, seemed redundant for instrumental music, particularly in the jazz genre. However, the streaming landscape has brought about significant changes. Andreas acknowledges the transformation, noting that his background in the pop world has helped him adapt to these changes. With the adoption of single strategies, he emphasizes the importance of precise timing, content creation, and building an environment around releases (ibid.).

Heartcore Records has also been using the "single strategy." Since early 2020, the label, under the guidance of representative Kurt Rosenwinkel, has been releasing at least two singles prior to each album launch. This calculated move is designed to create anticipation, engage audiences, and build momentum leading up to the full album release. They actively engage in discussions with their distributor, The Orchard, to explore and implement new, effective planning approaches. The distributor, relying on the metadata provided by the label, executes these plans, ensuring a successful release process (interview with the author, January 9, 2023). Similarly, Dave Douglas' Greenleaf relies on their distributor's (Red Eye Worldwide) efforts to promote music within the DSPs (interview with the author, February 23, 2023). A very similar case was described by Ray Jafford, whose label Razdaz Recordz newly collaborates with the distribution company Believe (interview with the author, September 22, 2021).

One of the pivotal elements in Heartcore Records' strategy is the emphasis on "marketing highlights," as pointed out by the label's representative Kurt Rosenwinkel. The label recognizes the importance of providing comprehensive and compelling marketing information to facilitate successful pitching processes. This strategic approach arms The Orchard with the necessary tools to effectively present Heartcore's releases to digital platforms and their curators, enhancing the visibility and reach of their artists. The recent success of a Swedish jazz trio album secured long-term placement in the popular "Jazz Chill" playlist on Apple Music. This accomplishment not only boosted the artist's visibility but also generated substantial income. Encouraged by this success, Heartcore Records remains motivated to refine its strategies, raising the chances of playlist placements in its expanding catalog (interview with the author, January 9, 2023).

Matti Nives, representing We Jazz Records, embraces a dynamic approach to the evolving music landscape, particularly in the digital realm. He emphasizes the significance of utilizing singles as part of their strategy, expressing, "*We definitely use singles. And we definitely try to play the streaming game.*" Recognizing the value of playing the streaming game effectively, Nives expresses joy in witnessing tracks perform well on streaming platforms. He underlines the importance of continuous learning, stating, "*The digital realm is not something that we just kind of have there and ignore; we always try to learn how to do that better.*" For Nives, meaningful engagement across various formats is crucial, reflecting the beauty of the modern age. He highlights the diversity of music discovery available through platforms like Spotify and Bandcamp, noting that the abundance of good music allows for a broad exploration across genres. From Nives' perspective, this adaptability to multiple digital platforms and a commitment to meaningful engagement represent key facets of navigating the contemporary music landscape (interview with the author, April 19, 2022).

In response to the question about using tools from streaming services like Spotify for Artists, Freifeld Tontraeger's Alexander Yannilos acknowledges the utilization of these tools within his approach. He emphasizes the importance of maintaining a credible and authentic profile on Spotify, drawing parallels to the necessity of a well-curated social media presence. Yannilos recognizes Spotify's Artist page as a kind of social media platform, underlining the significance of having an appealing profile with a good image, relevant information, and potential tour dates or lyrics, particularly in the context of pop music (interview with the author, April 26, 2022).

While he actively engages with these tools to enhance the artist's digital presence, Yannilos candidly expresses a sense of uncertainty regarding the metrics and data provided. He notes that while he observes a notable audience from Sweden, interpreting these numbers and translating them into actionable strategies remains a challenge for him. This candid reflection suggests a nuanced perspective on the role of streaming analytics, indicating a need for further exploration and understanding of how such data can be effectively leveraged in the context of his work (ibid.).

In response to the question about using singles and pre-releases on streaming services, Alexander Yannilos acknowledges the possibility but highlights the substantial promotional efforts required to create anticipation. He notes that when he's not actively involved in the albums, the album is always being released at once, emphasizing the potential need for a PR person to handle such promotional activities. Yannilos shares his proactive approach by advocating for the production of a video showcasing the album, emphasizing the value of capturing studio moments, especially for live-recorded music. He believes that dedicating time to film these moments pays off and aims to ensure there's at least one impressive video before the album release to enhance promotion. Regarding the practice of pre-saving albums or promoting singles before release, Yannilos expresses uncertainty about its significant impact on the overall outcome. He believes that a cross-platform video, shareable on social media, holds similar value. Currently, his label does not actively pursue pre-saving albums or promote singles in this manner, but he remains open to the possibility in the future (interview with the author, April 26, 2022).

In response to questions about releasing singles, Vojta Drnek explains that his label Ma Records, which is of a similar size to Yannilos's, primarily utilizes Bandcamp for single releases. Unlike Yannilos, Drnek's label does not use Spotify for Artists' pitching tools, primarily because they often release debut albums, and the absence of an existing artist profile precludes the use of these services. While the promotion of singles does occur, it largely hinges on the individual artist's initiative and activity. Drnek's approach reflects a reliance on the artists to drive their promotional efforts, indicating a more artist-centric model where the label provides the platform, but the artists play a significant role in their own promotion (interview with the author, December 10, 2021).

Werner Aldinger from Enja Records expresses a perspective on marketing within the realm of streaming platforms, highlighting his recognition of the need for a fresh perspective from a younger generation. He articulates a belief that someone younger, perhaps 30–40 years his junior, would be better suited to navigate the future pathways of jazz distribution in the digital field. While Aldinger acknowledges his ongoing efforts to stay informed about current trends, such as pitching for singles, he humbly admits that his role doesn't position him as the torchbearer for future developments. He emphasizes the importance of a transition into the future for Enja Records, suggesting that the task is beyond his scope, and he hopes to find someone capable of steering the label through the evolving landscape of digital music distribution. Aldinger underscores the value of Enja's established name and structure as a solid foundation for future endeavors but acknowledges that the torch of innovation must be passed to the younger generation for optimal adaptation to the evolving music industry landscape (interview with the author, February 15, 2023).

3.2.5.2 Marketing on Social Media

Andreas Brandis adopts a comprehensive approach to social media promotion, recognizing the digital nature of the younger generation and their primary engagement on platforms like social media and streaming services. Despite the presence of a following on these platforms, Brandis acknowledges the challenges in converting it into a substantial fan base. He highlights the necessity of considerable effort, especially with newcomers, stating that the initial investment in marketing for a debut release can surpass the conventional 10–20 percent of the expected turnover. For well-established artists, the strategy may differ, relying on leveraging existing recognition and promoting new releases with high-quality content. Brandis emphasizes the longer perspective in this approach, acknowledging that the investment in the first record sets the stage for subsequent releases to gain traction. Notably, he sheds light on the holistic view of marketing, considering factors like headcount, personnel roles, and specific investments in advertisement ads and Facebook campaigns, constituting a significant portion, ranging from 10 to 50 percent, of the overall marketing strategy (interview with the author, May 13, 2022).

In his promotional strategies, Dave Douglas of Greenleaf utilizes targeted post boosts for small advertisements. Additionally, approximately once a week, the label leverages the reach of Bandcamp by releasing newsletters, often featuring announcements of upcoming events, including Zoom interviews organized by Dave Douglas with diverse artists. This multifaceted approach underscores the label's commitment to utilizing various platforms for engagement and promotion. Bandcamp serves as a central hub for disseminating information about these events, fostering direct connections with the fan base, and highlighting the label's adaptability in utilizing digital spaces for effective communication and community building (interview with the author, February 23, 2023).

Kurt Rosenwinkel and Heartcore Records take an active stance on social media, finding notable success with organic reach. During the COVID-19 pandemic, they engaged their audience with humorous video content specifically featuring Kurt Rosenwinkel, some of which went viral. This success stemmed from spontaneous rather than meticulously planned strategies. For other artists on the label, they create regular content and teasers to maintain engagement. While they occasionally invest in social media ads, Rosenwinkel notes that the results often do not justify the expenditure. Instead, the label thrives on organic engagement, leveraging creative content that resonates naturally with its audience for long-term promotional impact. Additionally, Heartcore Records utilizes newsletters and has recently started a TikTok account, where they repost much of the content created for Instagram. They aim to expand their campaigns by developing TikTok-specific content in the future, recognizing the platform's growing influence (interview with the author, January 9, 2023).

Matti Nives emphasizes the community aspect of Bandcamp, viewing it as a social media platform in its own right. Nives highlights the mutual benefits for labels, artists, and music fans who actively engage on Bandcamp. By participating in discussions and staying involved in the Bandcamp community, labels can foster a deeper connection with their audience, promoting their music in a more integrated and interactive manner. This approach underscores the value of being an active participant in the music community to enhance visibility and engagement (interview with the author, April 19, 2022).

Alexander Yannilos stresses the importance of social media for pushing content and engaging with journalists and other key industry figures. His approach blends online promotion with in-person networking, such as meeting journalists at concerts and keeping them informed about the label's activities. Yannilos believes in a collaborative effort between the label and the artists, working together rather than the label shouldering all promotional responsibilities. This partnership model aims to ease the promotional burden on artists while ensuring they remain actively involved in their own marketing efforts. For social media, Yannilos focuses heavily on Instagram for engagement and Facebook for event promotion, particularly for release concerts, which can significantly impact album sales (interview with the author, April 26, 2022).

Vojta Drnek highlights the significant role of Facebook in the Czech Republic, where his label has the largest following. The label mirrors its Facebook content on

Instagram, striving to build a community on both platforms. Additionally, Drnek aims to cultivate a Bandcamp community similar to Greenleaf and We Jazz Records, recognizing the platform's potential for fostering direct connections with fans. This strategy indicates a multi-platform approach, balancing between established social media giants and niche music communities to maximize reach and engagement (interview with the author, December 10, 2021).

3.2.5.3 PR: Magazines and Reviews

The prevailing trend among the majority of responding labels indicates a preference for traditional marketing channels, particularly when a budget is allocated for promotional activities. These labels commonly invest in traditional avenues such as printed and electronic magazine placements, radio placements, and securing reviews in specific territories. While digital platforms have become increasingly influential, the surveyed labels predominantly continue to allocate resources to time-tested traditional marketing strategies, leveraging the effectiveness of print media, radio, and localized reviews.

Werner Aldinger recognizes the value of traditional marketing investments. While he values advertisements and placements in magazines, he acknowledges that the cost of PR services in traditional print media is presently higher compared to digital marketing alternatives, including social media ads. This recognition suggests a pragmatic awareness of the economic considerations and changing dynamics in the marketing sphere. Aldinger's determination is to "*keep up with all the new ways of marketing in the digital field and physical world*" (interview with the author, February 15, 2023).

Andreas Brandis from ACT Music anticipates a significant paradigm shift in the music industry, foreseeing a time when offline advertising diminishes and traditional jazz magazines face extinction. He emphasizes the unique impact and strong following of these monthly publications like *Downbeat*, *Jazz Mag*, and *Jazz Thing*. Brandis acknowledges the symbiotic relationship between labels and these magazines, with marketing efforts heavily invested in sustaining them. However, he acknowledges the inevitable transition towards increased digital marketing, even expressing a degree of reluctance in the face of what he considers the potential drawbacks of data science-based advertisement. Despite reservations, Brandis recognizes the advantage of direct communication with the audience through digital channels, underscoring the looming transformation in the industry's promotional landscape (interview with the author, May 13, 2022).

Heartcore Records adopts a mixed PR strategy, investing in traditional services for certain projects. The label hires a publicist to distribute press releases and secure placements in traditional jazz-oriented music magazines and radio stations. This investment is primarily motivated by the goal of supporting the booking of shows for the bands whose albums are being released. By leveraging traditional PR, Heartcore Records aims to enhance the visibility and credibility of its artists, facilitating broader opportunities for live performances (interview with the author, January 9, 2023).

Similarly, We Jazz Records, under the guidance of Matti Nives, also engages in project-based funding for PR activities. They allocate resources for specific campaigns, such as their current initiative for PR in Germany, enabling them to hire local publicists and run advertisements. These targeted efforts are part of broader export-oriented projects that include the UK, U.S., and Germany. We Jazz Records also runs a quarterly magazine, which has grown into a significant component of their promotional strategy. This publication not only promotes their music but also helps them connect with various music scenes, suggesting that the magazine might become a central financial operation for the label (interview with the author, April 19, 2022).

Greenleaf Music, led by Dave Douglas, takes a collaborative approach to PR by encouraging artists to hire their own publicists. Douglas believes that having a publicist is crucial for the artists' career advancement and prefers that artists use their releases as "platforms" for their next creative steps. While Greenleaf Music does engage in hiring publicists, they emphasize the importance of artist-driven marketing efforts. Douglas notes the shrinking space for this genre of music in print media and highlights the role of radio campaigns, especially in the U.S., where college radio remains a significant outlet. However, he acknowledges the uncertainties and limited impact of some digital platforms and smaller websites that would publish the albums' press releases and/or reviews (interview with the author, February 23, 2023).

Freifeld Tontraeger, managed by Alexander Yannilos, relies on personal connections for PR. Yannilos sends promotional copies to journalists he meets at live events, as the label does not have a budget for hiring agencies. This approach emphasizes direct engagement and relationship-building over formal PR campaigns. Similarly, Ma Records also handles media outreach in-house, collaborating with artists to build a media list for their mailouts. This strategy allows both labels to maintain a personal touch in their promotional efforts, leveraging existing networks and relationships to gain media coverage (interview with the author, April 26, 2022).

3.2.5.4 Event Marketing

Hevhetia's marketing and PR efforts benefit from collaborations with foreign partners and distributors. The Summer Music Festival is a pivotal period, backed by notable grants from governmental institutions, generating substantial interest and website traffic through content sharing and fan engagement on social media. Live streaming and the label's YouTube channel, featuring full-length videos of festival concerts, further amplify their reach (interview with the author, February 12, 2023).

At ACT Music, efforts have been made to celebrate anniversaries with concerts designed to foster a sense of community among the audience. For example, a concert was hosted at the Berlin Philharmonic, following the 25th Jubilee concert in

2017 at the Concert House in Denmark. The latter event sold out twice on the same day, attracting attendees from Germany, France, Austria, Switzerland, Scandinavia, and Finland. This widespread dedication to ACT Music indicates that fans are connected not only to individual artists but to the label as a whole (interview with the author, May 13, 2022).

Freifeld Tontraeger has highlighted the role of release concerts in impacting an album's success, sometimes accounting for the majority of its sales. Even albums that do not perform well in the catalog can benefit from a well-executed release show. Historically, release shows were organized at various venues depending on specific performance needs, such as the quality of music instruments. Initially managed by Alexander Yannilos, these events provided a high level of service but became increasingly challenging due to the close collaboration with musicians and the accompanying promotional expectations. Despite the rewards, the approach was demanding in terms of both time and energy (interview with the author, April 26, 2022).

We Jazz Records has operated as a limited company, handling the label and record shop alongside freelance work in radio and writing. An association was also established to organize festivals, facilitating easier funding in Finland. The core team comprises four full-time employees, with additional part-time staff and trainees. The festivals, including the original We Jazz Festival and the newer Odysseus Festival in the summer, have become important meeting points for those interested in the label's releases. These events provide opportunities to engage with the audience and showcase both label bands and other musicians (interview with the author, April 19, 2022).

At Greenleaf Music, the community is engaged through various initiatives, such as a podcast where musicians are interviewed about their work, extending beyond the label's artists. Additionally, a monthly label hang on Zoom has been hosted since the pandemic, featuring discussions on music, track plays, and interactions with subscribers. These sessions, which are recorded and archived for subscriber access, foster a sense of community and connection among fans (interview with the author, February 23, 2023).

Ma Records also organizes an annual festival, Ma Fest in Prague, that features artists from their catalog, fostering a sense of community and encouraging mutual support among artists in their artistic endeavors (interview with the author, December 10, 2021).

In summary, the marketing and PR strategies of these music labels demonstrate a strong emphasis on community building and audience engagement. Collaborations with foreign partners and digital platforms are leveraged to extend reach during major music festivals. Anniversaries are celebrated with significant concerts that foster a sense of community among fans. Release concerts are highlighted as crucial for album success, despite the organizational challenges they present. Festivals serve as important meeting points for fans and musicians, providing opportunities for engagement and showcasing talent. Community engagement is further enhanced through podcasts and monthly online sessions. Annual festivals also play a key role in fostering a supportive artistic community. Each label employs unique event marketing tactics to create memorable experiences and deepen connections with their audiences.

Conducted Interviews

Alexander Yannilos (Freifeld Tontraeger), (interview with the author, April 26, 2022).
Andreas Brandis (ACT Music), (interview with the author, May 13, 2022).
Dave Douglas (Greenleaf Music), (interview with the author, February 23, 2023).
Ján Súdzina (Hevhetia), (interview with the author, February 12, 2023).
Kervin, M. Dockendorf (Fangtasia Music), (interview with the author, June 26, 2023).
Kurt Rosenwinkel (Heartcore Records), (interview with the author, January 9, 2023).
Kyle McEvoy (Sonder House, Only One on the Mountain), (interview with the author, March 28, 2024).
Matti Nives (We Jazz Records), (interview with the author, April 19, 2022).
Naemi Wetter (The Orchard), (interview with the author, July 16, 2024).
Ray Jafford (Razdaz Recordz), (interview with the author, September 22, 2021).
Vojta Drnek (Ma Records), (interview with the author, December 10, 2021).
Werner Aldinger (Enja Records), (interview with the author, February 15, 2023).

Other Sources

Cole, T. (2010). You ask, we answer: What exactly is a 360 deal? NPR. https://www.npr.org/sections/therecord/2010/11/24/131574836/you-ask-we-answer-what-exactly-is-a-360-deal?t=1650279435162
Creative Law & Business. (2024). 360-deals. Creative Law & Business. https://creativelaw.eu/newsandblog/360-degree-deals-a-label-perspective
Hutchison, T. W., Strasser, R., & Hull, G. P. (2011). *The Music business and recording industry: Delivering Music in the twenty-first century*. Routledge.
IFPI. (2024). *Global music report 2024*. IFPI. https://ifpi-website-cms.s3.eu-west-2.amazonaws.com/IFPI_GMR_2024_State_of_the_Industry_db92a1c9c1.pdf
iMusician. (2021). What is happening with the Vinyl Industry? iMusician. https://imusician.pro/en/resources/blog/whats-happening-with-the-vinyl-industry
Luckerson, V. (2016). 11 albums that are missing from Spotify. Time. https://time.com/4274430/spotify-albums/
Sax, D. (2016). *The revenge of analog: Real things and why they matter*. Public Affairs.
Smith, M. D., & Telang, R. (2017). *Streaming, sharing, stealing: Big data and the future of entertainment*. MIT Press.
Tschmuck, P. (2021). *The economics of music*. Newcastle upon Tyne: Agenda Publishing.
Weatherbed, J. (2024). *Spotify leaks suggest lossless audio is almost ready*. The Verge. https://www.theverge.com/2024/5/3/24147887/spotify-hifi-lossless-audio-music-streaming-ui-leak
Whines, E. (2023). Garth Brooks explains why his music will never be on Spotify or Apple Music. Countrytown. https://countrytown.com/news/garth-brooks-explains-why-his-music-will-never-be-on-apple-spotify/8qBI5Ofm6eg/15-03-23

Chapter 4
Conclusion and Discussion

Abstract In this concluding chapter, the synthesis of key findings addresses the research questions central to this research, providing an analysis of the characteristics and operational strategies of independent jazz micro-labels. The investigation reveals that these labels typically operate on a small scale, prioritize artistic integrity, and support authentic artistic expression. They cater to niche markets, cultivating loyal fan bases and diversifying revenue streams through physical and digital sales, live performances, merchandise, and crowdfunding. Despite the challenges of adapting to digital distribution, these labels employ innovative strategies, leveraging both traditional and digital platforms to sustain their operations. This chapter delves into how independent jazz micro-labels balance artistic values with commercial realities, ensuring their resilience and continued relevance in the contemporary music industry.

The sections that follow in this chapter provide an in-depth exploration of the conclusions drawn from the research, answering the individual research questions posed at the outset. Firstly, the chapter discusses the characteristics of independent jazz micro-labels, highlighting their unique operational models and community-focused approaches. Following this, the discussion on financial, product, distribution, and marketing strategies outlines how these labels navigate their market conditions, emphasizing both their innovative practices and areas for improvement. Furthermore, the adaptation to technological advancements is explored, showcasing the shift from previous resistance to proactive engagement with digital tools and platforms. Finally, the chapter concludes with reflections on the awareness and utilization of available income channels, tools, and trends by these labels, summarizing their strategies to sustain and thrive in a competitive industry.

M. Drnek Bóková, *Strategies of Micro-Enterprises in the Recording Industry*, Music Business Research, https://doi.org/10.1007/978-3-031-88439-9_4

4.1 What Are the Characteristics of Independent Jazz Micro-Labels?

As defined in this book, independent jazz micro-labels typically operate on a small scale, employing fewer than ten people. This small size allows for flexibility and adaptability, enabling them to respond quickly to changes and opportunities in the industry, but can also be limited by the lack of funds and human resources. These labels prioritize artistic integrity and creative freedom, often supporting authentic artistic expression and maintaining a strong community focus. They cater to niche markets, providing personalized support to artists and cultivating loyal fan bases that major labels might overlook. To sustain their operations, these labels diversify their revenue streams. They often rely on income from other related or unrelated businesses, live performances, merchandise sales, crowdfunding, grants, and digital audio or video sales and streaming. Despite the market's trend of decreasing physical sales, they also adopt unique product strategies, offering a mix of traditional formats like CDs and vinyl records along with digital releases on their own webshops, Bandcamp, and traditional streaming platforms. Sometimes, the labels are experimenting with unique formats such as cassette tapes, single vinyls, and limited editions. Some labels exist thanks to the voluntary work of enthusiasts, do not generate any income for the company, and serve mostly as a tool to publish and present music of a certain community.

Despite their innovative approaches, independent jazz micro-labels face several challenges, particularly in fully adapting to the digital age. Logistical complexities in digital distribution can hinder their operations. While they increasingly leverage digital tools and platforms for distribution and marketing, using social media and digital marketing strategies to reach broader audiences, the transition from physical to digital formats remains complex. Additionally, these labels must manage operational challenges without the extensive resources available to larger labels. Some European labels work on a project basis, getting governmental support for their artists to sustain the production expenses. Nevertheless, their focus on artistic integrity, community building, and innovative strategies allows them to navigate the modern music industry effectively, preserving and promoting jazz music in a rapidly evolving landscape.

4.2 What Product, Distribution, Marketing, and Financial Strategies Do the Independent Micro-Companies in Jazz Choose for Their Activities?

Independent jazz micro-companies employ a variety of strategies to navigate their unique market conditions. These strategies, however, often diverge from recommended industry trends, revealing both strengths and areas for improvement.

4.2.1 *Financial Strategies*

Diversifying revenue streams is crucial for financial sustainability. This includes income from physical and digital sales, live performances, merchandise, and licensing deals for films, video games, and other media. Crowdfunding and grants are significant sources of funding, and effective financial management is essential for handling royalties and maintaining cash flow.

What Labels Do

Interviews show that labels diversify their revenue streams by incorporating mostly physical and digital sales. Small operations rarely get involved in live performances or licensing deals. Some of them use crowdfunding and grants to finance projects and engage in volunteer-based operations to minimize costs and maximize resources. Some labels have created additional digital and/or physical products to sustain their businesses.

Gaps

The literature highlights the significant impact of digital technologies, which have made the creation and distribution of music more cost-effective but also led to a decline in high-revenue physical sales like CDs. Labels have responded by cutting back on big budgets and artist advances. There is a growing emphasis on licensing music for films, TV shows, commercials, and video games as a crucial revenue stream. Major labels have adopted 360-degree deals to share profits from various income streams, including live performances, merchandise, and corporate sponsorships.

Interviews with digital distributors emphasize the future importance of digital and long-tail royalties, recognizing platforms like TikTok, Spotify, and Apple Music as primary revenue sources. Smaller, consistent income from micro-sync deals and collaborations/remixes to boost streaming numbers are highlighted as effective strategies. Flexible contracts where artists retain publishing rights and own their masters are seen as more sustainable and appealing.

Despite recognizing the importance of digital streams, the interviewed labels could further capitalize on digital and long-tail royalties. Investing more in understanding and optimizing digital revenue channels could enhance their sustainability. Additionally, some labels could benefit from a more aggressive pursuit of licensing deals, particularly in media like film, TV, and video games. This can provide substantial revenue streams and increase artist visibility.

While crowdfunding is being used, it is not universally or consistently applied across projects. More systematic use of crowdfunding can help labels secure upfront funding, reduce financial risk, and engage with fans directly. Labels can develop more robust crowdfunding strategies, offering unique incentives and experiences to backers.

Most labels refrain from involving themselves in artists' income beyond record sales. Although resource-intensive, adopting elements of 360-degree deals could help labels support artists comprehensively and share in diverse revenue streams, such as merchandise, live performance revenues, and sponsorships.

A more strategic use of social media to create viral content and engage new audiences could significantly boost streams and sales. Labels need to invest in digital marketing expertise and tools to enhance their online presence and engagement.

Exploring more innovative financial models, such as flexible artist contracts, micro-sync deals, and digital content monetization (e.g., online courses, exclusive digital releases), could provide new revenue streams and artist support mechanisms. Some EU-based labels use grants extensively, while others are moving away from them to maintain artistic freedom. More consistent and strategic use of grants, combined with private sponsorships and partnerships, could provide stable funding without compromising artistic vision.

Developing more cost-effective production methods or exploring novel physical formats, such as limited editions and unique packaging, could attract collectors and increase margins. Further diversification into complementary revenue channels such as artist management, merchandise, and publishing rights could stabilize and grow income. Labels should consider a more integrated approach to artist services.

Greater collaboration and networking with other labels, artists, and industry stakeholders could create synergies, share resources, and open new opportunities for revenue and exposure. Platforms for collaborative projects and shared services could be developed.

4.2.2 Product Strategies

Industry trends advocate for a focus on digital formats, as streaming has significantly boosted overall recording industry income, now accounting for 67 percent of total revenues. Despite the growing dominance of digital formats in the music market, physical media retains its value within the jazz niche. Moreover, physical sales have shown an increase over the past 3 years (IFPI, 2024).

According to Dockendorf, licensing has become a crucial revenue stream, contributing significantly to the income of independent labels. Wetter emphasizes the importance of utilizing data analytics from streaming platforms to tailor marketing strategies and enhance audience engagement. Additionally, the viral spread of music on social media platforms has become pivotal, with TikTok playing a significant role. McEvoy highlights the strategy of remixes and collaborations with other artists to trigger the algorithm on streaming services and gain more streams.

What Labels Do

According to interviews, independent jazz micro-labels are successfully producing both physical and digital formats, recognizing the enduring value of CDs and vinyl records. One repeatedly mentioned reason for manufacturing CDs is also their value for the reviewers, radios, and magazines, who are asked to review or mention the album through their media.

They often experiment with unique physical formats, like limited-edition releases, despite acknowledging that the small margins on vinyl make profitability challenging. Most labels place their albums on streaming services but are flexible and willing to honor an artist's preference against such placement.

They also tend to offer high-quality downloads for their audiophile customer base and plan on adding more exclusive material. One of the labels, Greenleaf Music, has adopted subscription-based access to its entire catalog via Bandcamp.

The repertoire of the responding labels is not influenced by the current trend of remixing pre-existing tracks, but they do support collaborative projects. Some label representatives mentioned that these collaborations are driven by artistic vision and authenticity rather than commercial purposes. A highly popular distribution technique among the responding labels is the single-release strategy, which has been widely adopted.

In addition to recorded music, the labels have developed a variety of other products, including music charts, educational video materials, and textile products.

Gaps

The recording industry's current landscape is dominated by streaming services, which account for the majority of total revenues and have become an essential platform for reaching broad audiences. Despite this, the resurgence of physical formats like CDs and vinyl records highlights a continued demand for tangible music experiences. Independent jazz labels have recognized the importance of these formats, catering to audiophiles and collectors who value sound quality and physical packaging. However, while these labels acknowledge the significance of streaming, their strategies often reflect a cautious acceptance rather than full enthusiasm. This hesitation may prevent them from fully leveraging digital marketing and engagement opportunities.

Statistics reveal that while physical formats have seen a resurgence, streaming remains the primary revenue driver for the recording industry. Labels need to balance the high costs and logistical challenges of producing physical formats with the necessity of maintaining a strong digital presence. Currently, some labels delay streaming releases to prioritize physical sales, but this approach might miss the chance to engage with a broader, digital-first audience. To address this issue, labels could develop more comprehensive digital strategies, including exclusive streaming content and targeted playlists, to attract and retain younger listeners.

Furthermore, the digital realm offers vast potential beyond mere availability. Independent jazz labels should explore innovative uses of digital platforms, such as interactive fan experiences, live-streamed concerts, and exclusive behind-the-scenes content. Integrating blockchain technology could also provide more transparent and fair compensation for artists, addressing ongoing concerns about royalty distribution.

Labels are expanding their product offerings to include merchandise, educational content, and music charts in addition to recorded music, diversifying revenue streams and strengthening connections with fans. While these initiatives are promising, there's room for broader and more innovative product offerings.

Subscription-based models for exclusive content, personalized fan experiences, and interactive educational materials could further enhance fan engagement and loyalty.

4.2.3 Distribution Strategies

For distribution, the labels are leveraging both physical and digital channels effectively. Direct sales through their websites and at performances remain crucial, while partnerships with specialized distributors can enhance physical and digital reach. Utilizing platforms like Bandcamp is particularly beneficial for direct-to-fan sales, and maintaining a strong presence on streaming services like Spotify and Apple Music is essential given that streaming now constitutes 67 percent of global music industry revenues (MIDiA Research, 2024). Additionally, centralizing sales operations through a single distributor can streamline processes and reduce inefficiencies. With independent labels accounting for approximately 35 percent of the global music market (IFPI, 2023), these strategies collectively ensure a robust and diversified distribution approach.

What Labels Do
The interviews reveal that labels effectively use both physical distribution networks and distribute through digital streaming platforms like Spotify and Apple Music, as well as other providers such as Bandcamp and their own online shops. Some have made efforts to optimize their presence on streaming services through playlist pitching and managing artist profiles on DSPs.

Four of the responding labels highlighted the importance of partnerships with their contracted distributor; some of them recently switched to a different distributor, expecting more efficient services in the field of physical, but especially digital distribution.

Independent jazz micro-labels employ a variety of physical distribution strategies, from direct sales via their websites to partnerships with distributors for broader reach. They also maintain physical sales through concerts and tours, highlighting the importance of direct fan engagement. Challenges persist, such as the reduction in physical distributors and high shipping costs.

Due to the decline in physical sales over the last two decades of the twenty-first century, two pre-1990 labels have reduced their reliance on local distributors, leading to a shift towards centralizing sales. They now aim to streamline operations by fulfilling orders worldwide through a single channel.

The same issue arises with digital distribution; having multiple distributors for streaming services can lead to inefficiency and chaos. Managing metadata and summarizing reports for each territory is complicated, making it more effective to have one global distributor for DSPs, according to label representatives. Some of these labels utilize aggregators like DistroKid, CD Baby, and Amuse, while some partner with larger distributors to enhance their digital footprint. Platforms like Bandcamp are pivotal for D2F sales and community building, with a strong emphasis on accurate metadata management to avoid last-minute issues.

All of the responding labels sell their physical product (or let their artist sell the product) at the live events of the artist or the label's events.

Gaps

The literature on music distribution highlights the evolving landscape, emphasizing the role of both physical and digital channels. Traditional physical distribution, once dominated by major labels through chain stores and niche outlets, has seen a resurgence in vinyl and CD sales due to nostalgia and high-profile releases. Digital distribution, however, has become paramount, with platforms like Bandcamp and SoundCloud offering direct sales and community engagement. Digital Service Providers (DSPs) such as Spotify, Apple Music, and Deezer are crucial for reaching wider audiences, necessitating strategic playlist pitching and robust analytics to optimize visibility and engagement.

Interviews with digital distributors reveal significant operational challenges, including last-minute delivery of masters and incorrect file submissions. Labels often lack coherent strategies, leading to haphazard releases. External pressures, such as the acquisition of independent distributors by major labels, further complicate the landscape, reducing the effectiveness of independent operations. Larger distributors like The Orchard and Believe offer advantages, including better deals with DSPs, higher payout rates, and personalized support. Future trends indicate a move towards direct distribution models that bypass traditional intermediaries, simplifying the process for artists and labels.

Despite the strides made in digital distribution, gaps remain in the strategies of independent jazz micro-labels. There is often a lack of comprehensive planning, leading to poorly timed releases. Metadata management and technical preparation need improvement to ensure smooth distribution processes. While platforms like Bandcamp are effectively utilized, optimizing presence on DSPs through playlist pitching and enhanced artist profiles could further boost visibility. Additionally, addressing physical distribution challenges through more efficient shipping solutions or strategic partnerships can alleviate logistical complexities.

4.2.4 Marketing Strategies

Successful marketing strategies heavily rely on digital tools and platforms. Social media (especially TikTok) and digital marketing tools are essential for engaging audiences and promoting releases. Utilizing streaming platforms for marketing, including playlist pitching and featuring artists on popular playlists, is critical. Traditional marketing methods like PR campaigns and event marketing should complement digital efforts. It is also important to mention the access to data provided by Spotify for Artists.

What Labels Do

Interviews with industry insiders reveal that while there is a growing emphasis on digital marketing strategies, physical product marketing is not entirely disregarded.

Digital sales have become a substantial part of the music industry income, reflecting the shift towards online platforms. However, the recent resurgence in physical music sales underscores the continued relevance of traditional marketing methods. Many labels outsource physical product marketing to contractual distributors, highlighting a balanced approach that prioritizes digital strategies while still acknowledging the importance of physical sales. Event marketing, including release concerts and festivals, is also employed to foster community engagement and boost album sales.

In response to the transformative shifts in the music industry, independent labels are developing tailored marketing strategies to thrive in the digital realm. Labels working with distributors often focus on collaborative efforts to enhance their digital presence, including pitching, playlisting, and promotional campaigns on major streaming platforms. The adoption of single release strategies has become more prevalent, aimed at building anticipation and engaging audiences before album launches. Labels also emphasize social media engagement, utilizing platforms like Instagram, Facebook, and Bandcamp to connect with audiences. Traditional marketing avenues, such as printed and electronic magazine placements and radio placements, remain in use, particularly when budgets allow. Overall, the dynamic and adaptive nature of modern music industry marketing is evident in the blend of digital, physical, and community building efforts employed by record labels.

Gaps

According to the literature, effective marketing strategies encompass a comprehensive plan that includes product identity, pricing, promotion, advertising, and sales, with a strong emphasis on digital marketing. This involves leveraging social media platforms like Facebook, Instagram, and TikTok for event promotion, visual content, and viral marketing. Additionally, streaming platforms play a crucial role through playlist pitching, SEO, music licensing, and optimized artist profiles, supported by targeted advertising such as Spotify ads to enhance audience engagement and revenue streams (Bodde, 2023).

Insights from digital distributors underscore the importance of advanced strategies within streaming platforms and social media. They highlight the potential of TikTok ads, purchasing promotional spaces on DSPs like Spotify and Apple Music, and maintaining well-managed artist profiles across all platforms. These strategies, combined with organic growth through collaborations and community building on platforms like Facebook, WhatsApp, and Discord, offer a multifaceted approach to marketing. The emphasis is on genuine connections over paid ads, driving external traffic to DSPs, and leveraging new features like Spotify's Canvas and Marquee for enhanced visibility and engagement.

In contrast, the interviewed independent jazz micro-labels exhibit varying degrees of adoption and effectiveness in these areas. While some labels like ACT Music, Heartcore Records, and We Jazz Records have embraced the singles strategy and collaborative efforts with distributors for playlisting and pitching, others face challenges due to limited access to pitching systems and reliance on aggregators. There is also a noticeable gap in the comprehensive use of digital marketing tools, with many labels expressing uncertainty about interpreting streaming analytics and the effectiveness of paid advertising.

Moreover, as highlighted by Naemi Wetter, there is an overreliance on Spotify and neglect of other DSPs like Deezer and Tidal. The underutilization of advanced DSP features and tools further hampers visibility and engagement. Labels also show a preference for traditional PR investments and limited integration of digital strategies. The importance of community building and data-driven marketing is often overlooked, leading to missed opportunities for engagement and optimized campaigns.

4.3 Entrepreneurs' Adaptability

Dias and Medbøe (2014) Claim that Representatives of the Jazz Genre Rather Lag, and Even Resist, Change and Are Unwilling to Adapt to Evolving Technological Progress. What Do the Independent Jazz Micro-Labels Do Today to Adapt to the Ever-Changing Industry?

Dias and Medbøe (2014) claimed that representatives of the jazz genre often lagged behind and resisted technological changes. However, the current practices of independent jazz micro-labels reflect a significant shift from this perspective, showing a proactive adaptation to the evolving digital landscape. Initially hesitant about streaming platforms due to concerns over low royalty rates and transparency, many jazz labels have now embraced these platforms to reach broader audiences, particularly younger listeners who predominantly consume music digitally.

Independent jazz micro-labels have adopted various strategies to enhance their digital presence and maximize their reach. For instance, labels like Greenleaf Music utilize Bandcamp for its supportive community and direct-to-fan sales model, integrating subscription services to build a dedicated listener base. Similarly, Heartcore Records and Razdaz Recordz have partnered with distributors like The Orchard and Believe to improve their digital distribution and gain better playlist placements, aiming to increase their visibility and engagement online. Additionally, some labels focus on offering high-fidelity digital products, catering to audiophiles who value superior sound quality, which helps attract and retain loyal fans.

Despite challenges in vinyl production, many independent jazz labels continue to include vinyl LPs in their catalogs due to their popularity among jazz enthusiasts. Labels like We Jazz Records have found success with vinyl singles, appealing to collectors and maintaining a niche market. These labels also diversify their offerings to include merchandise, music charts, and educational video products, providing additional revenue streams and enhancing their brand image.

However, while these labels have made considerable strides, they are still somewhat slow in catching up with the newest trends. The financial constraints and smaller operational scale of independent jazz labels make it challenging to adopt the latest technological advancements as quickly as larger labels. This lag is evident in areas such as advanced data analytics for marketing or the swift adoption of emerging digital platforms.

Moreover, independent jazz labels are forming strategic partnerships with global aggregators to streamline digital distribution and manage the complexities of metadata and promotional efforts. For example, ACT Music works with Kontor New Media to handle digital distribution efficiently. At the same time, labels like Greenleaf Music focus on community building on platforms like Bandcamp, directly engaging with their audience.

In conclusion, independent jazz micro-labels have evolved significantly from the resistance to technological change noted by Dias and Medbøe (2014). By embracing digital distribution, maximizing digital reach, offering high-quality products, diversifying their offerings, and forming strategic partnerships, these labels demonstrate a dynamic and resilient approach to navigating the challenges of the digital age. However, their limited resources mean they are still somewhat slow in catching up with the latest trends, underscoring the ongoing need for innovation and adaptation in this ever-changing industry.

4.4 Entrepreneurs' Awareness

Are the Independent Jazz Micro-Labels Aware of the Available Income Channels, Tools, and Trends, and Are they Using Them?

Today, independent jazz micro-labels are actively engaging with digital and streaming strategies, although not all are catching up equally. Most of the labels have adapted to the single strategy, and involve tools such as Spotify for Artists to pitch their releases to playlists. Labels like ACT Music work closely with distributors such as Kontor New Media to handle pitching, playlisting, and promotional campaigns across multiple platforms. This collaboration highlights the strategic decision-making involved in optimizing digital distribution efforts. Similarly, Heartcore Records, under Kurt Rosenwinkel's guidance, releases singles prior to album launches to build momentum and engage audiences. Their partnership with The Orchard ensures the execution of these plans, supported by detailed marketing information to facilitate successful pitching to digital platforms.

We Jazz Records's Matti Nives and Dave Douglas of Greenleaf Music leverage Bandcamp's direct-to-fan model and subscription services to build a dedicated listener base while relying on contracted distributors for broader physical and digital promotion. We Jazz Records actively plays the "streaming game" by releasing singles and engaging with digital platforms to enhance their visibility. Freifeld Tontraeger's Alexander Yannilos emphasizes maintaining an authentic profile on Spotify and utilizing streaming tools, although he acknowledges the challenges in interpreting data for actionable strategies but does not involve a single release strategy for lack of resources.

Not all interviewed labels are fully catching up with current trends in the digital and streaming sphere. There is a lack of plans to reach younger audiences by investing in social media and digital advertising. Platforms like Instagram, TikTok, and Facebook are essential for creating engaging content that resonates with modern listeners. This lag is often attributed to limited resources, which make it challenging for smaller labels to adopt the latest technological advancements as quickly as larger counterparts. Financial constraints and smaller operational scales mean that some labels struggle to implement advanced data analytics for marketing, extensive use of artificial intelligence in music recommendation systems, and the swift adoption of emerging digital platforms.

In conclusion, independent jazz micro-labels have made significant strides in adapting to the digital age, embracing streaming platforms, and diversifying their marketing strategies. However, the adoption of the latest trends varies, often due to resource limitations. While some labels are successfully navigating the digital landscape with innovative approaches, others face challenges in keeping up, underscoring the ongoing need for adaptation and innovation in this ever-changing industry.

Sources

Bodde, E. (2023). *Utilizing social media platforms in music marketing*. Tampere University of Applied Sciences.

Dias, J., & Medbøe, H. (2014). Improvisation in the digital age: New narratives in jazz promotion and dissemination. *First Monday, 19*(10). https://doi.org/10.5210/fm.v19i10.5553

IFPI. (2023). Engaging with music 2023. IFPI. https://www.ifpi.org/wp-content/uploads/2023/12/IFPI-Engaging-With-Music-2023_full-report.pdf

IFPI. (2024). Global music report 2024. IFPI. https://ifpi-website-cms.s3.eu-west-2.amazonaws.com/IFPI_GMR_2024_State_of_the_Industry_db92a1c9c1.pdf

MIDiA Research. (2024). Music streaming services subscribers market shares 2023. Music Industry Blog. https://www.statista.com/statistics/653926/music-streaming-service-subscriber-share/

Research Limitations

This book provides a focused examination of a few companies within a specific genre niche based on qualitative data from semi-structured interviews. While this method captures the historical behavior of these companies in the 2020s, it lacks the quantitative data necessary for longitudinal comparisons.

The author also suggests that comparing these companies' trends with those in other genres could provide valuable context. Furthermore, the study does not differentiate labels by age, territory, or size. Future research could benefit from examining various types of labels, such as new versus long-established, one-person versus team-run, and those with extensive catalogs versus emerging ones. Such distinctions could reveal unique challenges and strategies that may be overlooked when focusing on a homogeneous sample. Despite the global reach of the labels studied, local communication significantly impacts their strategies, an aspect not addressed in this research.

The study explores only four functional-level strategies, leaving many other management strategies unexamined. The limitations of semi-structured interviews constrain the depth of insights into each strategy. Therefore, the author encourages future researchers to focus on individual strategies for a more comprehensive understanding of the product, marketing, distribution, and financing practices of jazz micro-labels. This approach could provide deeper insights and foster a better understanding of the diverse strategic approaches within the jazz music industry.

M. Drnek Bóková, *Strategies of Micro-Enterprises in the Recording Industry*, Music Business Research, https://doi.org/10.1007/978-3-031-88439-9

Personal Observations

While working on this book, I have gained and shared many different perspectives on the strategies and challenges faced by micro-labels in the jazz recording market. This exchange of ideas has been incredibly enlightening. Even though industry dynamics might imply a competitive relationship, there is a strong sense of collaboration driven by our shared goal of nurturing and sustaining a niche genre amidst other financially and marketing-wise stronger genres.

Having managed Kurt Rosenwinkel's Heartcore Records since 2016, I have witnessed firsthand the crucial role that collaboration and partnerships play in the success of independent labels. I am convinced that independent jazz labels can significantly expand their reach and resources by forming alliances with other labels, artists, and industry stakeholders. These collaborations lead to joint marketing efforts, shared distribution networks, and collective bargaining power, which are essential for navigating the complexities of the modern music landscape.

Moreover, the importance of data-driven decision-making cannot be overstated. Utilizing data analytics to understand audience preferences, optimize release schedules, and tailor marketing strategies can provide independent labels with a competitive edge. This approach not only enhances the effectiveness of their efforts but also ensures that they are meeting the evolving demands of their listeners.

While independent jazz micro-labels exhibit a strong commitment to artistic integrity and community, there is ample opportunity for them to adopt more innovative and aggressive strategies seen in other music genres. Addressing the limitations of this study by expanding the informant base and incorporating more diverse perspectives will provide a richer understanding of the strategies employed across the industry.

My experience managing Heartcore Records has reinforced the necessity of these strategic approaches. The insights gained while working on this research have had a positive influence on my decision-making and helped to implement strategic thinking to ensure the longevity and prosperity of our independent jazz label in today's dynamic music landscape.

M. Drnek Bóková, *Strategies of Micro-Enterprises in the Recording Industry*, Music Business Research, https://doi.org/10.1007/978-3-031-88439-9

Attachments

Attachment 1: The Model Questionnaire for Representatives of Independent Jazz Micro-Labels (The Author)

The Model Questionnaire for Representatives of Independent Jazz Micro-Labels

Strategies of Micro-Enterprises in the Recording Industry with a Focus on Independent Jazz Record Labels

Informants' Definition:

1. Managers/CEO of independent labels belonging to the group of micro-companies (less than ten employees)
2. Marketing and distribution departments of independent labels belonging to the group of micro-companies
3. Entrepreneurs running independent labels belonging to the group of micro-companies

Informants:

Alexander Yannilos—Freifeld Tonträger (AT)—2015
Andreas Brandis—ACT Music (DE)—1992
Dave Douglas—Greenleaf Music (USA)—2005
Ján Súdzina—Hevhetia (SK)—2002
Kurt Rosenwinkel—Heartcore Records (US/DE)—2016
Matti Nives—We Jazz Records (FI)—2016
Ray Jafford—Razdaz Recordz (UK)—2002
Vojta Drnek—Ma Records (CZ)—2020
Werner Aldinger—Enja Records (DE)—1971

M. Drnek Bóková, *Strategies of Micro-Enterprises in the Recording Industry*, Music Business Research, https://doi.org/10.1007/978-3-031-88439-9

Results Expected After Compiling the Questionnaires:
Answers to questions (qualitative data):

- What are the primary income channels for the independent micro jazz labels?
- Do these labels overlap with other branches of the music industry (live performance, licensing) and create 360-degree deals?
- What is the attitude of these labels to the digitalization and streaming industry?
- Do they use tools that are available in the current music industry?
- What are the functional strategies of these labels concerning the significant change in the industry?
- Is there a common trend in functional strategies that these labels share?
- How do the current strategies influence the repertoire?

Other analysis:

- Mapping of distribution strategies
- Mapping of product strategies
- Mapping of marketing strategies (crucial changes in marketing strategies—retail marketing, online marketing, direct marketing)
- Way of digital distribution and its development in individual jazz micro-labels
- Notice when jazz micro-labels started to adapt to the streaming services and what is/was their way of adapting to the market
- Streaming services and small labels now (playlist pitching, charts)—which tools are they using the most
- Mapping label's unique approaches

Sections:

Section One—Introduction—Characteristics of jazz micro-labels
Section Two—Financial aspects and strategies
Section Three—Product aspects and strategies
Section Four—Distribution aspects and strategies
Section Five—Marketing aspects and strategies

Questions:
Section One—Introduction—Specification of the label

1. Year of the establishment
2. What made you (or the label's founder) start the label?

Section Two—Financial aspects and strategies

3. What kind of departments of the artist's development does your label administer and take a percentage from?

   (a) Only revenues from master usage (CD, LP, Digital)
   (b) Live performance
   (c) Merchandising
   (d) Licensing
   (e) Other (specify)

4. What is the most crucial channel of your funding?
    (a) Sales income
    (b) Crowdfunding
    (c) Private sponsor
    (d) Governmental support/Grants
    (e) Different

Financial Strategy

5. Do you plan to invest less or more in different segments (marketing, distribution, product) in the following years?

Section Three—Product aspects and strategies

6. What *kind of product* does your label produce?
    (a) Only digital
    (b) Only physical
    (c) Digital and physical
    (d) Merchandising
    (e) Other (specify)
7. What kind of *physical* product does your label produce?
    (a) CD
    (b) LP
    (c) CD and LP
    (d) Merchandising
    (e) Other

Influence of the Strategies on Repertoire

8. Has the digital distribution changed your artistic approach to the productions, considering the length, volume, etc., of the tracks?
9. Do you pick different genres than jazz in your releases?
10. Do you use featured artists on your albums?
11. Do you produce remixes of your albums?

Product Strategy

12. What do you consider to be the current trends related to the product in the recording industry?
13. What kind of product formats are you planning to focus on the most?
14. Do you plan to change your approach to products in the five following years?

Section Four—Distribution aspects and strategies
Physical Distribution

15. Do you distribute physical products in retail stores?
16. Do you use the D2F fulfillment service for your D2F orders?
17. Do you have your own online/retail store?

Relationship to streaming services

18. Do you publish your music on streaming services?
19. What is your opinion about streaming services?
20. Have you ever refused to publish your album on streaming services?
21. When (year) did you publish your first album (or transfer the complete catalog) at any streaming platform?

Digital Distribution

22. How do you distribute your digital albums (aggregators such as Distrokid, TuneCore, and CD Baby…, distributor)?
23. Has the way of distribution changed since your first digital release?

Distribution Strategy

24. What do you consider to be the current trends in physical distribution in the recording industry?
25. What do you consider to be the current trends in digital distribution in the recording industry?

Section Five—Marketing aspects and strategies

26. How much percent of the budget of one project do you invest in marketing one release on average?
27. Do you invest in digital marketing?
28. What roles have singles in your release plans?
29. What do you focus on the most significantly while promoting your albums?
30. Do you consider your customer base a community?
31. Do you develop your community through social media/streaming services?

Marketing Strategy

What do you consider to be the current trends in marketing in the recording industry?

Attachment 2: The Model Questionnaire for Representatives of Digital Distribution Sector

The Model Questionnaire for Representatives from the Digital Distribution Sector

Strategies of Micro-Enterprises in the Recording Industry with a Focus on Independent Jazz Record Labels

Informants:

- Owners and/or managers of companies providing digital distribution

- Kervin M. Dockendorf
- Kyle McEvoy
- Naemi Wetter

Results Expected After Compiling the Questionnaires: Answers to questions (qualitative data):

1. Identification of Effective Income Channels in the Digital Realm
   - Insights into which digital income channels are deemed most effective for record labels
2. Best Practices for Maximizing Revenue
   - Strategies and tools within streaming services that artists and labels should focus on to enhance visibility and competitiveness
   - Effective marketing and advertising approaches on social media and streaming platforms
3. Challenges and Solutions in Label-Distributor Collaboration
   - Common mistakes and challenges faced by labels in their collaboration with distributors
   - Practical solutions and best practices for better planning and execution of releases
4. Strategic Planning for Independent Labels
   - Recommendations for independent labels on budget allocation for marketing and investment in various types of marketing
   - The balance between passion for music and economic viability in signing and promoting artists
5. Future Trends and Adaptation
   - Perspectives on the future of physical sales versus digital royalties, especially for niche genres like jazz
   - Creative strategies for repurposing existing music to generate additional revenue and maintain relevance in the digital era

Questions:

1. In your opinion, which channels of income are the most effective for record labels, particularly in the digital space?
2. In the world of digital music distribution, what should artists and labels focus on to maximize their opportunities?
3. What specific tools within streaming services can help artists increase their visibility and competitiveness?
4. What are the most common mistakes labels make in their collaboration with distributors, and how can these be avoided?

5. What advice would you give to independent jazz micro-labels to help them succeed in the digital era?
6. How should independent labels allocate their budget for marketing, and what types of marketing should they invest in?
7. What are the pros and cons of working with different types of distribution companies, such as major labels, independent distributors, and accessible platforms like Distrokid or CD Baby?
8. What unique advantage does your distribution company offers compared to larger or more accessible distribution services?
9. What is your perspective on the future of physical sales versus digital royalties for jazz labels?

References

Interviews

Werner Aldinger (Enja Records), (interview with the author, February 15, 2023).
Andreas Brandis (ACT Music), (interview with the author, May 13, 2022).
Kervin M. Dockendorf (Fangtasia Music), (interview with the author, June 26, 2023).
Dave Douglas (Greenleaf Music), (interview with the author, February 23, 2023).
Vojta Drnek (Ma Records), (interview with the author, December 10, 2021).
Ray Jafford (Razdaz Recordz), (interview with the author, September 22, 2021).
Kyle McEvoy (Sonder House, Only One on the Mountain), (interview with the author, March 28, 2024).
Matti Nives (We Jazz Records), (interview with the author, April 19, 2022).
Kurt Rosenwinkel (Heartcore Records), (interview with the author, January 9, 2023).
Ján Súdzina (Hevhetia), (interview with the author, February 12, 2023).
Naemi Wetter (The Orchard), (interview with the author, July 16, 2024).
Alexander Yannilos (Freifeld Tontraeger), (interview with the author, April 26, 2022).

Bibliography

Act Music. (2024). *About ACT*. ACT Music Official Website. https://www.actmusic.com/en/About-ACT/ACT-Music
Ahmed, A., & Tammet, D. (2023). Bandcamp lays off half its staff after buyout by Songtradr. *The Guardian*. https://www.theguardian.com/music/2023/oct/17/bandcamp-lays-off-half-its-staff-after-buyout-by-songtradr
Amos, M. (2023). Which country has the biggest music industry in 2023? *RouteNote*. https://routenote.com/blog/which-country-has-the-biggest-music-industry-in-2023/
Anderton, C., Dubber, A., & James, M. (2013). *Understanding the music industries*. Sage.
Arditi, D. (2021). *ITake-over: The recording industry in the streaming era*. Lexington Books.
Bačuvčík, R. (2010). *Jak posloucháme hudbu? Vztah obyvatel České republiky k hudbě a jejímu poslechu 2009*. VeRBuM.
Bandcamp. (2020). *Ma Records. Ma Records: Music*. https://marecords.bandcamp.com/

M. Drnek Bóková, *Strategies of Micro-Enterprises in the Recording Industry*, Music Business Research, https://doi.org/10.1007/978-3-031-88439-9

Bandcamp. (2023). *We Jazz Records. We Jazz Records: Merch.* https://wejazzrecords.bandcamp.com/

Bandcamp Staff. (2024). This Friday is Bandcamp Friday. *Bandcamp Daily.* https://daily.bandcamp.com/features/bandcamp-fridays-in-2024

Bargfrede, A. (2017). *Music law in the digital age: Copyright essentials for Today's music business.* Berklee Press.

Bartmanski, D., & Woodward, I. (2020). *Labels: Making Independent Music.* Bloomsbury Academic.

BBC. (2018). How Spotify came to be worth billions. *BBC.* https://www.bbc.com/news/newsbeat-43240886

Bell, T. L., & Johansson, O. (Eds.). (2016). *Sound.* Society and the Geography of Popular Music.

bestrategicplanning.com. (2024). Different Levels of Strategy. *BeStrategicPlanning.* https://bestrategicplanning.com/different-levels-of-strategy/

Blauvelt, C. (2017). *The mysterious origins of jazz.* BBC. https://www.bbc.com/culture/article/20170224-the-mysetrious-origins-of-jazz

Bodde, E. (2023). *Utilizing social media platforms in music marketing.* Tampere University of Applied Sciences.

Brandis, A. (2024). *VITA. Andreas Brandis.* https://www.andreasbrandis.de/vita/

Browne, D. (2022). Cassette tapes are making a comeback. *Rolling Stone.* https://www.rollingstone.com/music/music-features/cassette-tape-comeback-walkman-1234606978/

Cambridge Dictionary. (2023). *INDEPENDENT | English meaning - Cambridge Dictionary.* Cambridge Dictionary. https://dictionary.cambridge.org/dictionary/english/independent

Cambridge University Press & Assessment. (2024). *STRATEGY | English meaning - Cambridge Dictionary.* Cambridge Dictionary. https://dictionary.cambridge.org/dictionary/english/strategy

Cannon, R. (2022). Beyond the headlines: Media representations of artist discourse on the artist-label relationship. **IASPM Journal, 12*(1). https://doi.org/10.5429/2079-3871(2022)v12i1.2en

Carter, E. (2024). Poverty among riches: understanding the contracted economy for recorded music and its impact on market actors. *Journal of Cultural Economy, 17*(3), 345–359. https://www.tandfonline.com/doi/abs/10.1080/17530350.2024.2302152

Catalano, T. J. (2023). Microenterprise: Definition, Types, Example - Business. *Investopedia.* https://www.investopedia.com/terms/m/microenterprise.asp

Christman. (2011). What Exactly Is An Independent Label? Differing Definitions, Different Market Shares. *Billboard.* https://www.billboard.com/music/music-news/what-exactly-is-an-independent-label-differing-definitions-1177068/

Cole, T. (2010). You Ask, We Answer: What Exactly Is A 360 Deal? *NPR.* https://www.npr.org/sections/therecord/2010/11/24/131574836/you-ask-we-answer-what-exactly-is-a-360-deal?t=1650279435162

Crane, D. (1976). Reward Systems in art, science and religion. *The Production of Culture, 19*(6), 57–62.

Creative Law & Business. (2024). 360-deals. *Creative Law & Business.* https://creativelaw.eu/newsandblog/360-degree-deals-a-label-perspective.

Daisie Team. (2023). Pros & Cons of Physical vs Digital Music Distribution. *Daisie Blog.* https://blog.daisie.com/pros-cons-of-physical-vs-digital-music-distribution/#pros-of-physical-music-distribution

Danko, M. (2021). Ján Sudzina z vydavateľstva Hevhetia: Financovanie hudby je dnes diskutabilné. *Hudba.sk.* https://hudba.zoznam.sk/rozhovory/25-10-2021-jan-sudzina-z-vydavatelstva-hevhetia-financovanie-hudby-je-dnes-diskutabilne/

Dechsakda, R. A. (2012). *The effects of digital music distribution.* Southern Illinois University Carbondale.

Deutsche Jazzunion. (2022). Jazzstudie 2022. *Deutsche Jazzunion.* https://www.deutsche-jazzunion.de/jazzstudie-2022/

Deutsches Musikinformationszentrum. (2023). *Bevorzugte Musikrichtungen nach Altersgruppen*. https://miz.org/de/statistiken/bevorzugte-musikrichtungen-nach-altersgruppen

Dias, J., & Medbøe, H. (2014). Improvisation in the digital age: New narratives in jazz promotion and dissemination. *First Monday, 19*(10). https://doi.org/10.5210/fm.v19i10.5553

Discogs. (2024). *Exploring Jazz on Discogs*. https://www.discogs.com/search/?ev=em_rs&genre_exact=Jazz

Europe Jazz Network. (2024). European Jazz Conference 2024: Tomorrow comes Today | Europe Jazz Network. *Europe Jazz Network*.https://www.europejazz.net/press-release/european-jazz-conference-2024-tomorrow-comes-today

European Commission. (2020). *User guide to the SME Definition*. Publications Office of the European Union.

Freifeld Tontraeger. (2022). Yannilos | Freifeld Tontraeger. *Freifeld Tontraeger*. https://www.freifeldtontraeger.com/yannilos

Galuszka, P., & Wyrzykowska, K. M. (2016). Running a record label when records don't sell anymore: Empirical evidence from Poland. *Popular Music, 35*(1), 23–40. https://doi.org/10.1017/S0261143015000811

Gammons, H. (2011). *The art of music publishing: An entrepreneurial guide to publishing and copyright for the music, film and media industries*. Focal Press.

George, T. (2022). Semi-Structured Interview | Definition, Guide & Examples. *Scribbr*. https://www.scribbr.com/methodology/semi-structured-interview/

Gioia, T. (2017). *How to listen to jazz*. Basic Books.

Gray, H. (1983). *Producing jazz: The experience of an independent record company*. Temple University Press.

Greenleaf Music. (2005–2024). About. *Greenleaf Music by Dave Douglas*. https://greenleafmusic.com/

Greenwood, C. (2023). *Spotify profits 2.0: Music marketing and business strategies for the new singles economy*. Chris Greenwood.

Guo, X. (2023). The evolution of the music industry in the digital age: From records to streaming. *Journal of Sociology and Ethnology, 5*(10). https://doi.org/10.23977/jsoce.2023.051002

Hatteau, B. (2011). Jazz news: ENJA Records' Matthias Winckelmann Interviewed at All About Jazz! *All About Jazz*. https://www.allaboutjazz.com/news/enja-records-matthias-winckelmann-interviewed-at-all-about-jazz/

Havers, R. (2023). The history of recorded Jazz | uDiscover. *uDiscover Music*. https://www.udiscovermusic.com/in-depth-features/the-history-of-recorded-jazz/

Hayes, J. (2020). State of the Industry: Major Label vs. Non-Major Label Regional Performance. *Hypebot*. https://www.hypebot.com/hypebot/2020/01/state-of-the-industry-major-label-vs-non-major-label-regional-performance.html

Heartcore Records. (2023). About. *Heartcore Records Online Shop*. https://heartcore-records.com/#about

Hesmondhalgh, D. (1998). Post-punk's attempt to democratize the music industry: The success and failure of rough trade. *Popular Music, 16*(3), 255–274.

Hesmondhalgh, D. (2021). Is music streaming bad for musicians? Problems of evidence and argument. *New Media & Society, 23*(12), 3593–3615.

Hesmondhalgh, D., Jones, E., & Rauh, A. (2019). SoundCloud and Bandcamp as alternative music platforms. *Platformization of Cultural Production, 1*(13), 1–13. 11771/2056305.119883429.

Hevhetia. (2023). Official Website. *Hevhetia - Hevhetia*. https://www.hevhetia.com/

Hillier, N. (2023). Discover the Best Independent Jazz Labels|Bestofjazz.org. *Best of Jazz*. https://bestofjazz.org/the-best-independent-jazz-labels/#full

Hitters, E., & den Drijver, R. (2017). The Business of DIY. Characteristics, motives and ideologies of micro-independent record labels. *Cadernos de Arte e Antropologia, 6*(1), 17–35. https://doi.org/10.4000/cadernosaa.1192

Hull, T. (2004). *Jazz Labels. Tom Hull's Village Voice Review Drafts*. https://tomhull.com/ocston/arch/vv/labels-05.php

Hutchison, T. W., Strasser, R., & Hull, G. P. (2011). *The music business and recording industry: Delivering music in the 21st century*. Routledge.

IFPI. (2023). Engaging with music 2023. *IFPI*. https://www.ifpi.org/wp-content/uploads/2023/12/IFPI-Engaging-With-Music-2023_full-report.pdf

IFPI. (2024). Global music report 2024. *IFPI*. https://ifpi-website-cms.s3.eu-west-2.amazonaws.com/IFPI_GMR_2024_State_of_the_Industry_db92a1c9c1.pdf

iMusician. (2021). What is happening with the vinyl industry? *iMusician*. https://imusician.pro/en/resources/blog/whats-happening-with-the-vinyl-industry

Initiative Musik. (2024). *Initiative Musik*. Startseite. https://www.initiative-musik.de/

inJazz. (2024). *About injazz*. https://www.injazz.nl/about/

jazz | English meaning - Cambridge Dictionary. (2023). *Cambridge Dictionary*. https://dictionary.cambridge.org/dictionary/english/jazz

Jazz at Lincoln Centre. (2024). Mission & Values. *Jazz at Lincoln Center*. https://jazz.org/about-us/mission-values/

Jazz Finland. (2021). MATTI NIVES starts a new experimental music program on YLE. *Jazz Finland*. https://jazzfinland.fi/news/matti-nives-starts-a-new-experimental-music-program-on-yle

Jazzahead. (2024). About Us. *jazzahead! — jazzahead!*https://jazzahead.de/about-us/

Jazzforschung. (2024). *Jazz Encounters*. Institut 16 Jazzforschung. https://jazzforschung.kug.ac.at/events/veranstaltungen-des-instituts-fuer-jazzforschung/konferenzen/jazz-encounters

KBV Research. (2021). Music Streaming Market Size, Share & Forecast 2020–2026. *KBV Research*. https://www.kbvresearch.com/music-streaming-market/

Kees, I. N. (1998). The compact disc story. *JAES, 46*(5), 458–460. 462, 464, 465.

KEF. (2024). Hidden Mavericks of Music: Notable Indie Record Labels You Need To Know. *Sound of Life*. https://www.soundoflife.com/blogs/mixtape/indie-record-labels

Key Record Label Marketing Strategies [Recent Analysis]. (2023). *The Gitnux Blog*. https://blog.gitnux.com/strategies/record-label-marketing-strategies/

Kordestani, M. (2022). What Is the Role of a Record Label in Today's Music Business? *Rolling Stone*. https://www.rollingstone.com/culture-council/articles/what-is-the-role-of-record-label-in-todays-music-business-1234588863/

Krueger, A. (2020). *Rockonomics: What the music industry can teach us about economics (and our future)*. Hodder & Stoughton.

Kumpunen, N. (2022). *Sources of income for independent record labels*. Tampere University of Applied Sciences. https://www.theseus.fi/bitstream/handle/10024/752634/Kumpunen_Nestori.pdf?sequence=3&isAllowed=y

Kurt Rosenwinkel. (2023). Official Website. *Kurt Rosenwinkel*. http://www.kurtrosenwinkel.com

Kwon, J. (2020). Where is Jazz going?: reissues, Jazz Industry, and the future of Jazz | FUSION. *FUSION Magazine*. https://www.fusionmagazine.org/where-is-jazz-going-reissues-jazz-industry-and-the-future-of-jazz/

Kwon, J. (2022). Freedom and control: Musicians' a ol: Musicians' autonomy and record labels' influence in producing the sound of contemporary jazz. In *Washington university open scholarship*. Washington University in St. Louis. https://openscholarship.wustl.edu/cgi/viewcontent.cgi?article=3783&context=art_sci_etds

Leea, M., Choia, H. B., Choa, D., & Lee, H. (2016). Cannibalizing or complementing? The impact of online streaming services on music record sales. *Elsevier B.V. T, 91*, 662–671.

Luckerson, V. (2016). 11 Albums That Are Missing From Spotify. *Time*. https://time.com/4274430/spotify-albums/

Lynch, R. (2018). *Strategic management*. Pearson Education Limited.

Macy, A., Rolston, C. P., Allen, P., & Hutchison, T. W. (2016). *Record label marketing: How music companies brand and market artists in the digital era*. Focal Press.

Maxwell, E. (2020). *Modernization of music*. Modernization of Music.

McCain, A. (2023). 30+ Harmonious Music Industry Statistics [2023]: Worth, Data, and Revenue. *Zippia*. https://www.zippia.com/advice/music-industry-statistics/

Meeder, C. (2012). *Jazz: The basics*. Taylor & Francis.

Meltzer, D. (Ed.). (1993). *Reading Jazz*. Mercury House.

Micro Business Development Program | Department for Children and Families. (2023). *Vermont Department for Children and Families (DCF)*. https://dcf.vermont.gov/benefits/MBDP

MIDiA Research. (2024). Music streaming services subscribers market shares 2023. *Music Indrustry Blog*. https://www.statista.com/statistics/653926/music-streaming-service-subscriber-share/

Monson, I., Early, G., & American Academy of Arts & Sciences. (2019). Why jazz still matters. *Daedalus, 148*(2), 7. 10.1162.

Moore, M. J. (2021). In 2021, jazz went back in time to see the future. *NPR*. https://www.npr.org/2021/12/20/1064066269/in-2021-jazz-went-back-in-time-to-see-the-future

Morgen, B. A. (2022). Optimisation of musical distribution in streaming services: Third-party playlist promotion and algorithmic logics of distribution. In G. Morrow, D. Nordgård, & P. Tschmuck (Eds.), *Rethinking the music business: Music contexts, rights, data, and COVID-19*. Springer International Publishing. https://doi.org/10.1007/978-3-031-09532-0_9

Mortimer, J. H., Nosko, C., & Sorensen, A. (2012). Supply responses to digital distribution: Recorded music and live performances. *Information Economics and Policy, 24*(1), 3–14. ISSN 0167-6245.

MRC. (2021). 2020 MRC Data Year-End Charts. *MCR Data Year-End Report U.S. 2020 Presented in Collaboration with Billboard*, 53.

Murphy, C. J. (2022). Spotify Canvas: Increase Your Track Shares by 145%. *Digital Music News*. https://www.digitalmusicnews.com/2022/03/07/spotify-canvas/

Music & Copyright. (2021). UMG and SME put the market share squeeze on WMG and the independent sector. *Music & Copyright's Blog*. https://musicandcopyright.wordpress.com/2021/04/21/umg-and-sme-put-the-market-share-squeeze-on-wmg-and-the-independent-sector/

Music & Copyright. (2023). Market Share—Music & Copyright's Blog. *Music & Copyright's Blog*. https://musicandcopyright.wordpress.com/tag/market-share/

Music Metrics Vault. (2024). Most popular jazz artists on Spotify. *Music Metrics Vault*. https://www.musicmetricsvault.com/genres/jazz/339

Nielsen Music. (2018). Mid-Year Report U.S. 2018. *Nielsen*. https://www.nielsen.com/wp-content/uploads/sites/2/2019/04/us-midyear-music-report-2018.pdf

Nwagwu, W. E., & Akintoye, A. (2023). Influence of social media on the uptake of emerging musicians and entertainment events. *Information Development*, (January). https://journals.sagepub.com/doi/pdf/10.1177/02666669221151162

Office Of Advocacy. (2023). *Small business facts: The role of microbusiness employers in the economy*. U.S. Small Business Administration. https://advocacy.sba.gov/2023/03/07/frequently-asked-questions-about-small-business-2023/

Ose, S. O. (2016). Using excel and word to structure qualitative data. *Journal of Applied Social Science, 10*(2), 147–162. https://doi.org/10.1177/1936724416664948

Other Records Labels. (2022). *Record label marketing strategies - 25 practical concepts*. Other Record Labels.

Paine, A. (2022). Music Week. *Music Week*. https://www.musicweek.com/labels/read/independent-labels-market-share-set-to-increase-for-fifth-consecutive-year/086968

Paine, A. (2024). *ERA: CD sales increase for the first time in 20 years*. Music Week. https://www.musicweek.com/labels/read/era-cd-sales-increase-for-the-first-time-in-20-years/089068

Palm, M. (2017). Analog backlog: Pressing records during the vinyl revival. *Journal of Popular Music Studies, 29*. https://doi.org/10.1111/jpms.12247

Paul, A. S. (2019). Aggregation Services and Songwriter Independence. *Capstone Projects and Master's Theses* 680. https://digitalcommons.csumb.edu/caps_thes_all/680?utm_source=digitalcommons.csumb.edu percent2Fcaps_thes_all percent2F680&utm_medium=PDF&utm_campaign=PDFCoverPages

Pitt, I. L. (2015). *Direct licensing and the music industry: How technology, innovation and competition reshaped copyright licensing*. Springer International Publishing.

Preece, I. (2017). *Stats, records & rock 'n' roll: Fine-tuned Infographics to rock your world*. Carlton Books, Limited.

Priest, E. (2021). The future of music copyright collectives in the digital streaming age. *The Columbia Journal of Law & Arts, 45*(1) https://journals.library.columbia.edu/index.php/lawandarts/article/view/8953/4621

Prouty, K. (2012). *Knowing jazz: Community, pedagogy, and canon in the information age*. University Press of Mississippi.

Purdy, K. (2023). End of an era: CD Baby stops distributing artists' CDs, vinyl, and other goods. *Ars Technica*. https://arstechnica.com/culture/2023/05/end-of-an-era-cd-baby-stops-distributing-artists-cds-vinyl-and-other-goods/

Raffa, M. (2017). Jazz and the disc: Media, labels, producers. A century-long relationship. In *In a century of jazz. Impromptu creativity*. Skira. https://www.researchgate.net/profile/Massimiliano-Raffa/publication/361248599_Jazz_and_the_disc_media_labels_producers_A_century-long_relationship/links/62a5f1676886635d5cd41eb5/Jazz-and-the-disc-media-labels-producers-A-century-long-relationship.pdf

Razdaz Recordz. (2023). *About Us*. Razdaz Recordz. https://www.razdazrecordz.com/about-us/

Resnikoff, P. (2018). Collectively, Indie Labels are now bigger than any major label. *Digital Music News*. https://www.digitalmusicnews.com/2018/05/20/indie-labels-major-label/

RIAA. (2022). *U.S. music revenue database*. RIAA. https://www.riaa.com/u-s-sales-database/

Ricci, M. & Racci, V. (2021). Best jazz record labels article. *All About Jazz*. https://www.allaboutjazz.com/top-jazz-record-labels-2020

Richter, F. (2024). Infographic: Streaming drives global music industry to new highs. *Statista*. https://www.statista.com/chart/4713/global-recorded-music-industry-revenues/

Rodičová, J. (2015). Comparison of music preferences of university students in The Czech Republic and other European Union countries. *Music Preferences of Youth as a Contemporary Music Education Issue, 264*(26), 67–77. https://doi.org/10.5817/CZ.MUNI.P210-8108-2015

Rosen, P. (1997). It was easy, it was cheap, go and do it! Technology and anarchy in the UK music industry. In J. Purkis & J. Bowen (Eds.), *Twenty-first century anarchism. Unorthodox ideas for a new millennium.*

Ross, A. (2011). *Listen to this*. Fourth Estate.

SAEInstitute.(2023).*Returnofvinylandphysicalmusic|insights|SAEblog*.SAEInstitute.https://www.sae.edu/gbr/insights/the-return-of-vinyl-analysing-the-resurgence-of-physical-music-formats/

Samkova, M. (2020). *Interview with Ray Jefford, Manager to Avishai Cohen*. Jazzfuel. https://jazzfuel.com/interview-ray-jefford-avishai-cohen-manager/

Savage, M. (2022). More and more musicians are releasing their own music: Here's why. *BBC*. https://www.bbc.com/news/entertainment-arts-60051802

Sax, D. (2016). *The revenge of analog: Real things and why they matter*. Public Affairs.

Schafer, B. (2021). Where will spotify be in 5 Years? *The Motley Fool*. https://www.fool.com/investing/2021/04/15/where-will-spotify-be-in-5-years/

SeekingAlpha. (2013). Trans World Entertainment: Transformation In Decline. *Nasdaq*. https://www.nasdaq.com/articles/trans-world-entertainment-transformation-decline-2013-03-19

Semancik, A. (2024). *How AI is transforming the creative economy and music industry*. Ohio University. https://www.ohio.edu/news/2024/04/how-ai-transforming-creative-economy-and-music-industry

Smith, M. D., & Telang, R. (2017). *Streaming, sharing, stealing: Big data and the future of entertainment*. MIT Press.

Songtrust. (2023). MUSIC PUBLISHING GLOSSARY - Digital Service Provider (DSP). *Songtrust*. https://www.songtrust.com/music-publishing-glossary/glossary-digital-service-provider

Soundcharts Team. (2022). A Complete Guide to Music Distribution Companies. *Soundcharts*. https://soundcharts.com/blog/music-distribution

Spotify. (2021). *Five Things to Know About Spotify HiFi — Spotify*. *Spotify Newsroom*. https://newsroom.spotify.com/2021-02-22/five-things-to-know-about-spotify-hifi/

Spotify. (2024). Kyle McEvoy. *Spotify*. https://open.spotify.com/artist/6rRqxCKHpl9C5Imf2uinft

Spotify for Artists. (2024). Provider Directory—Spotify for Artists. *Spotify for Artists*. https://artists.spotify.com/providers

Statista. (2024). Global record companies market share 2023. *Statista*. https://www.statista.com/statistics/422926/record-companies-market-share-worldwide-physical-digital-revenues/

Stone, J. (2020). *The state of the music industry in 2020*. Toptal. https://www.toptal.com/finance/market-research-analysts/state-of-music-industry

Strachan, R. C. (2007). Micro-independent record labels in the UK: Discourse, DIY cultural production and the music industry. *European Journal of Cultural Studies, 10*(2), 245–262.

Taylor, T. D. (2015). *Music and capitalism: A history of the present*. University of Chicago Press.

The Intellectual Property Office. (2019). Music 2025: The music data dilemma: Issues facing the music industry in improving data management. *The Intellectual Property Office*.

Thomas, A. K. (2019). *Thinking in sync: A primer on the mind of a music supervisor*. Yay Team Productions, Incorporated.

Tsang, G. (2022). A peep at the current state of jazz music through data from Spotify (part 1). *George Tsang*. https://tsanggeorge.medium.com/a-peep-at-the-current-state-of-jazz-music-through-data-from-spotify-part-1-75400069f2dc

Tschmuck, P. (2006). *Creativity and innovation in the music industry*. Springer.

Tschmuck, P. (2021). *The economics of music*. Agenda Publishing.

Vigil, W. (2022). *Feb 26, 1917 CE: First jazz record released*. National Geographic Society. https://education.nationalgeographic.org/resource/first-jazz-record-released/

Vojta Drnek. (2023). *Vojta Drnek Bio*. Vojta Drnek | accordion. https://www.vojtadrnek.com/

Walzer, D. A. (2017). Independent music production: How individuality, technology, and creative entrepreneurship influence contemporary music industry practices. *Creative Industries Journal, 10*(1), 21–39.

Waring, C. (2021). Impulse For Change: A Short History of Impulse! Records. *uDiscover Music*. https://www.udiscovermusic.com/in-depth-features/story-of-impulse-records/

Warner, M. (2019). *Work hard playlist hard: The DIY playlist guide for artists and curators*. Tablo Publishing.

Weatherbed, J. (2024). Spotify leaks suggest lossless audio is almost ready. *The Verge*. https://www.theverge.com/2024/5/3/24147887/spotify-hifi-lossless-audio-music-streaming-ui-leak

Whines, E. (2023). Garth Brooks explains why his music will never be on spotify or apple music. *Countrytown*. https://countrytown.com/news/garth-brooks-explains-why-his-music-will-never-be-on-apple-spotify/8qBI5Ofm6eg/15-03-23

Wien Modern. (2022). Alexander Yannilos. *Wienmodern*. https://www.wienmodern.at/2022-bio-alexander-yannilos-de-3615

Wikipedia. (2019). Enja Records. *Wikipedia*. https://en.wikipedia.org/wiki/Enja_Records

Wikipedia. (2021). Werner Aldinger—Wikipedia. *Wikipedia*. https://de.wikipedia.org/wiki/Werner_Aldinger

Wikipedia. (2023). *Matti Nives*. https://fi.wikipedia.org/wiki/Matti_Nives

Wikström, P. (2014). *Ch@nge: The music industry in an age of digital distribution*. BBVA Open Mind. https://www.bbvaopenmind.com/wp-content/uploads/2014/04/BBVA-OpenMind-The-Music-Industry-in-an-Age-of-Digital-Distribution-Patrik-Wikstrom.pdf

Winter Jazzfest. (2024). Jazz Talks 2024 — Winter Jazzfest. *Winter Jazzfest*. https://www.winter-jazzfest.com/jazz-talks-2024

Witt, S. (2015). *How music got free: What happens when an entire generation commits the same crime?* Penguin Random House.

Worldwide Independent Network. (2022). Wintrends 2022. *Winformusic.org*. https://winformusic.org/mp-files/wintrends-2022.pdf/

The manufacturer's authorised representative in the EU is Springer Nature Customer Service Centre GmbH, Europaplatz 3, 69115 Heidelberg, Germany. If you have any concerns regarding our products, please contact ProductSafety@springernature.com

Printed and bound by CPI Group (UK) Ltd, Croydon, CR0 4YY
01/10/2026
02225977-0012